happy healthy ❖ baby cookbook ❖

happy healthy baby cookbook

nutritious, delicious and easy-to-prepare recipes
to give your child a healthy start in life

Sara Lewis

southwater

This edition is published by Southwater

Southwater is an imprint of Anness Publishing Ltd
Hermes House, 88–89 Blackfriars Road, London SE1 8HA
tel. 020 7401 2077; fax 020 7633 9499
www.southwaterbooks.com; info@anness.com

© Anness Publishing Ltd 1995, 2002
Published in the USA by Southwater, Anness Publishing Inc.,
27 West 20th Street, New York, NY 10011; fax 212 807 6813

This edition distributed in the UK by The Manning Partnership Ltd,
6 The Old Dairy, Melcombe Road, Bath BA2 3LR; tel. 01225 478 444;
fax 01225 478 440; sales@manning-partnership.co.uk

This edition distributed in the USA by National Book Network,
4720 Boston Way, Lanham, MD 20706; tel. 301 459 3366;
fax 301 459 1705; www.nbnbooks.com

This edition distributed in Canada by General Publishing,
895 Don Mills Road, 400–402 Park Centre, Toronto, Ontario M3C 1W3;
tel. 416 445 3333; fax 416 445 5991; www.genpub.com

This edition distributed in Australia by Pan Macmillan Australia, Level 18,
St Martins Tower, 31 Market St, Sydney, NSW 2000; tel. 1300 135 113;
fax 1300 135 103; email customer.service@macmillan.com.au

This edition distributed in New Zealand by The Five Mile Press (NZ) Ltd,
PO Box 33–1071 Takapuna, Unit 11/101–111 Diana Drive, Glenfield,
Auckland 10; tel. (09) 444 4144; fax (09) 444 4518; fivemilenz@clear.net.nz

A CIP catalogue record for this book is available from the British Library.

Publisher: Joanna Lorenz
Project Editors: Judith Simons and Emma Wish
Designer: Sue Storey
Special Photography: John Freeman
Stylist: Judy Williams
Home Economists: Sara Lewis, Jacqueline Clarke and Petra Jackson

Previously published as *What to Feed Your Baby*

1 3 5 7 9 10 8 6 4 2

NOTES

For all recipes, quantities are given in both metric and imperial measures and,
where appropriate, measures are also given in standard cups and spoons.
Follow one set, but not a mixture, because they are not interchangeable.

Standard spoon and cup measures are level.
1 tsp = 5ml, 1 tbsp = 15ml, 1 cup = 250ml/8fl oz

Australian standard tablespoons are 20ml. Australian readers should use 3 tsp
in place of 1 tbsp for measuring small quantities of gelatine, flour, salt, etc.

Medium eggs are used unless otherwise stated.

CONTENTS

INTRODUCTION

Introducing your baby to the delights of solid food heralds the beginning of a new and exciting stage in your baby's development. Although it will be a few months yet before your baby will be able to share in family meals fully, the foods that you give your baby now are vitally important not only for their nutritional benefits but also in laying down the first foundations for a healthy diet through childhood and beyond. There are several important factors to consider when planning your baby's diet: at what stage to begin

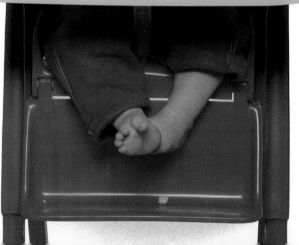

weaning; what foods to serve and when; and how to prepare foods quickly and easily while still providing the nutrient-dense diet babies need to support their rapid growth. Your baby's progression from milk feeds to solids will be gradual. Start with baby rice which is barely warm and only slightly thicker than milk, before moving on to those first few spoonfuls of smooth puréed vegetables and fruit. Then, stage by stage, you will be able to introduce your baby to a tempting array of new flavours and textures.

FIRST FOODS

Although during the first few years of any baby's life, food, diet and nutrition are vitally important – to build a healthy and energetic child and to develop good eating habits that will see the infant safely through childhood – there is a real shortage of reliable, practical information on the subject.

This book aims to outline all you need to know about feeding your baby. The book is packed with over 50 healthy recipes, all beautifully illustrated with colour pictures – from first purées, to finger foods and introducing those first tempting toddler meals.

In the very early days all a baby needs is milk, but as it grows so too will its nutritional needs. By four months most babies will have doubled their birth weight and will be ready to begin mini-mouthfuls of smooth purée.

Although this marks an exciting time in your baby's development it can also cause immense worry for a new parent. We all want to provide the best for our child and what better start in life than to begin laying the foundations for a healthy diet? But what do you do if your child won't eat, or just spits out those delicious spoonfuls of food that you have so lovingly prepared?

FIRST FOODS

This book covers everything you need to know about introducing those first few spoonfuls of smooth puréed foods: including when to begin weaning, the signs to look out for, what foods to serve and when, basic equipment, plus sound nutritional advice, helpful guidelines on food preparation and masses of colourful and exciting recipes to tempt your baby.

You will almost certainly find that helpful friends, relatives, health professionals and magazines will offer you differing and sometimes contradictory advice. Some will be genuinely useful, while some turn out to be outdated or inappropriate: the difficulty is sorting through the well-meaning confusion to find something reliable. This book has

Above: *Mediterranean Vegetables is just one of the delicious recipes to try.*

been based on information recently published by the British government in the Coma report *'Weaning and the Weaning Diet 1994'* and aims to offer helpful advice in accordance with this much-researched and authoritative document.

FOOD AND YOUR BABY

Childrens' nutritional needs are very different from our own. Forget about low fat, high fibre diets. Young children require nutrient-dense foods to meet their rapid levels of growth. Requirements for protein and energy are high in proportion to the child's size. Tiny tummies mean children are unable to eat large quantities of food while at the same time they are usually very active. Their appetites can vary enormously, but the range of foods that they will eat may also be very limited. So it is vital that the foods which are eaten contain a variety of nutrients, in combination with calories, while still fitting in with family meals. High fibre foods can be very filling without providing sufficient levels of protein, vitamins and minerals.

For young infants fat is the major source of dietary energy: both breast milk and infant formula contribute about 50% of energy as fat. As your child progresses to a mixed diet, the proportion of energy supplied by fat decreases and is replaced by carbohydrate. But it is important that the energy is provided by fat up to the age of two, as too much carbohydrate may be too bulky for a young infant.

Adequate energy is necessary to sustain growth. Fat is a very useful source of energy and the main source of the fat soluble vitamins, A, D, E and K, while also providing essential fatty acids that the body cannot make itself. It is best to obtain fat from foods which contain other essential nutrients, such as full-fat milk, cheese, yogurts, lean meat and small quantities of oily fish.

Try to include a portion of carbohydrate in every meal once your child is over nine months: for example bread, potatoes, rice or pasta for energy. Encourage young children to eat a variety of fruit and vegetables. As with adults, try to keep salt intakes to a minimum, and omit it altogether from home-prepared baby meals. Fried foods or very sugary foods should also be discouraged.

Obviously eating a healthy, well-balanced diet is essential for any age group, but social skills are also important. Our children learn from us and so it is also vital to eat together as a family, if not every day, then as often as possible, so that young children can discover not only how to behave at the table but also that eating is a sociable and enjoyable experience.

We do hope this book will make mealtimes fun for the entire family and help to minimize any problems and anxieties you may come up against when feeding your baby.

Above: *Start with simple vegetable purées at around four months.*

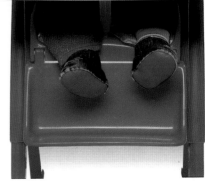

Right: *Babies are easily encouraged to take pleasure in their food, especially once they are able to help themselves!*

Weaning from Milk Feeds to Solids

Most babies are ready to begin those first few mini-mouthfuls of puréed foods at around four months and almost all babies will be eating solid food by six months. By this age babies need the extra energy, protein, iron and other essential nutrients that are found in solids in order to help them develop and grow. Your baby will also be progressing from sucking to biting and chewing – as many breast-feeding mothers find out!

Remember that every baby has individual needs, so don't be surprised if your baby seems ready for solids earlier or later than other babies of the same age. Don't feel pressurized by friends with young babies, or helpful relatives. Be guided by your own baby.

WHAT TO LOOK OUT FOR
- if your baby still seems hungry after a milk feed
- wants feeding more frequently
- starts waking at night after some weeks of sleeping through
- shows a real interest in the foods that you are eating
- seems more restless and grizzly

If your baby is showing some or all of these signs then she is probably ready to begin solids. Check with your health visitor; a few large and very hungry babies may show these signs earlier than four months, but the majority of babies should not be given solid foods before four months as their digestive systems can't cope.

Be guided as well by any family history of allergies, eczema or asthma. Studies suggest that babies who are fed on breast or formula milk that bit longer are less likely to develop these complaints.

In the early days of weaning, your baby is not dependent on solid food

Left: *When the signs are right, start your baby with a few mouthfuls of puréed food. Your baby will feel most comfortable seated on your lap at this stage, and adopting one of the positions you have used for breast feeding will enhance security and confidence.*

Below: *If you have any doubts or worries about the right time to try purées and solids, your nurse or health visitor will be able to help.*

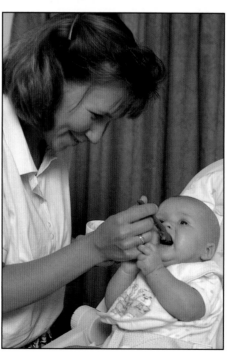

Above: *Your baby will very quickly take an interest in your hand and the spoon, and will play as she eats.*

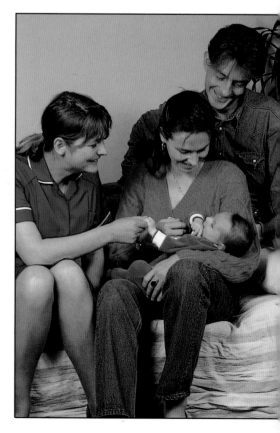

for the supply of nutrients as this is still met by milk feeds. Don't worry if she only takes a taste of food – the actual experience of taking food off a spoon is the important thing. However, by six months the baby's body store of nutrients has been used up and solid foods are crucial for supplying all the vital minerals and vitamins your baby needs.

WHAT ABOUT MILK FEEDS?

During the early stages of weaning, solids are given in addition to the normal feeds of breast or formula milk. As mixed feeding continues your baby will naturally cut down on the number of milk feeds, although milk will remain an important part of a child's diet.

Up to six months your baby should be having at least four milk feeds a day and by age one your baby needs at least 1 pint/600ml whole or full-fat milk a day. Milk will still be contributing 40 per cent of the energy she uses up.

More and more health professionals are now recommending that children should not be given cows' milk as their main drink until after 12 months, due to low levels of iron and vitamins C and D. Mothers are sometimes advised to go on to fortified formula when breast feeding has finished. Small amounts

Above: *Every baby is different. There is no need to be worried if your baby seems ready for solids earlier or later than other babies.*

of cows' milk may be used in cooking from six months, but it is better to use formula milk.

Full-fat cows' milk can be given to children between one and two, while semi-skimmed milk can be gradually introduced to those over two providing the child eats well. Skimmed milk should not be given to children under five.

Only give pasteurized milk to children. UHT or long-life milk is a useful standby for holidays and travelling as it doesn't need to be refrigerated, although once opened treat as full-fat pasteurized milk.

Some people prefer to give goats' or sheeps' milk feeling it is less allergenic and offers additional nourishment, although this cannot be substantiated. Goats' milk is deficient in folic acid and must not be given to babies under six months. Boil goats' milk before use, as it may be sold unpasteurized.

WEANING FROM BREAST OR BOTTLE

You can go on breast feeding your baby, as well as giving solid food, for as long as you wish. But many mothers are quite relieved when their baby is happy to try a feeder

cup or bottle along with their lunch-time "solid" meal.

Once solids become established the number of daytime milk feeds naturally tails off with just the special morning and evening comfort feeds continuing until you and baby are ready to stop.

Whether bottle or breast and bottle feeding, try to wean your baby off the bottle completely by the age of one. Otherwise your baby may find it difficult to give the bottle up and comfort sucking on a teat can be a hard habit to break.

Once your baby can sit up and is settled into three meals a day then you can introduce a lidded feeding cup. Initially at one meal a day, then at two and so on. But do make sure to cuddle your baby while giving a drink so that the baby still enjoys the closeness and security of being with mother or father. There may be a few setbacks when your baby is teething or unwell, but be guided by your baby.

Above: *Bottles are a wonderful aid; but try to wean your baby off them by age one, or the sucking habit can be difficult to break.*

Above: *It won't all happen at once: a mixed period of feeding with breast, bottle and simple solids is perfectly natural and healthy.*

Introducing Solid Food

Many parents find that around late morning, after their baby's morning sleep, is the best time to introduce solids. Baby is happy and nicely hungry without being frantic. Offer a small milk feed to take the edge off her immediate hunger and make her feel secure, and then go on to offer solid food. Finish with the rest of the milk feed or "second side".

SITTING COMFORTABLY

In the early days sit baby on your lap, protect her with a bib and yourself with a teatowel and hold the baby tightly so she feels secure. As you and baby become more confident about feeding then you may prefer to strap her into a portable car seat or baby chair. Most babies will be unable to sit in a highchair until six months or so.

FIRST SPOONFULS

First foods should be very smooth and mild in taste. Baby rice is often the most successful because its milky taste and soft texture seem vaguely familiar to the baby. Begin by trying a teaspoonful of bought baby rice, add a little previously boiled water, expressed breast milk or formula milk as the pack directs, and mix to make a smooth runny purée, slightly thicker than milk. Test the

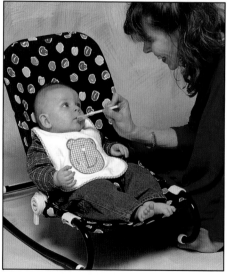

Above: *First baby rice will be barely warm, and only very slightly thicker than milk.*

Above: *At about six months your baby will be ready to sit safely in a highchair. You should always use a strap.*

Left: *A good interim stage between lap feeding and the highchair is a baby chair on the floor, or even a portable car seat.*

temperature on the edge of your lip, it should be just lukewarm – too hot and you may put baby off solids completely. Offer tiny amounts on the end of a sterilized teaspoon. Learning to eat from a spoon is quite a skill and your baby may start by spitting out the food until she has mastered the technique of taking food off the spoon and transferring it to the back of her mouth. Go at your baby's pace and don't try to hurry things. If your baby seems reluctant, then abandon the feed and go back to breast or bottle feeding. You could try solids again a few days later – there's plenty of time. Never force-feed and never add solid foods to a baby's bottle as it can lead to choking which can be dangerous.

Once your baby has accepted the idea of eating from a spoon continue with a midday meal of baby rice or

SPOON FEEDING FOR THE FIRST TIME

1 Sit your baby on your lap in a familiar position. Always test the temperature of the food.

2 Offer the spoon to your baby. Go slowly and if the spoon or food is rejected try again another day.

3 When your baby has taken its first solid food, sit quietly for a little while in an upright position.

puréed potato for a week or two to give her digestive system a chance to adjust to the new food.

After that, you could gradually introduce puréed carrot, parsnip and swede, or puréed dessert apple or pears. As always be guided by your baby: this is a slow process so don't try to hurry your baby if she is not ready or you will run the risk of putting her off altogether.

After three to four weeks your baby may be ready to try two mini meals a day. Increase the amount of food to 10 ml/2 tsp, even 15 ml/3 tsp if your baby seems ready. You may be able to slightly reduce the amount of formula or breast milk you use to make the purée so that it is not quite so sloppy.

If your baby likes the flavour, then offer it again for a few meals before introducing a new taste. If your baby spits out the food with obvious distaste then go back to baby rice or try mixing the new flavour with a little baby rice so that it is milder and more palatable.

Try to follow your baby's appetite and pace; most babies will stop when they have had enough. Don't be tempted to persuade your baby to finish off those last few spoonfuls.

It's a bad habit to make or encourage anyone to clear the plate if they are full. If you do it with a baby, she'll probably be sick!

Adopt a feeding schedule to suit you both. In the early days it may be easier to give baby breakfast before older children get up, or after they're at school, when the house is quieter.

Six to eight weeks into solid feeding and your baby will probably be ready for three small meals a day. But again be guided by her needs and appetite, so don't introduce a third meal until you feel she is really ready. Aim to feed your baby at roughly equal time intervals that will eventually coincide with as many family meals as possible.

TIPS
- Be guided by your baby and your health visitor.
- Sterilize all equipment before use.
- Don't force your baby if she doesn't seem ready for solids.
- Maintain milk feeds and offer plain boiled water or very diluted fruit juice as well.
- Try one taste at a time and continue with this until your baby is accustomed to it. If she doesn't like it, don't offer it for a few days.
- Remember, babies don't mind repetition, they've been living on milk for months!

Above: *Over the weeks you can build up the diet from baby rice to items like puréed carrot, parsnip, apple or pear, gradually leaving more texture as your baby seems ready.*

EQUIPMENT

Choose a small plastic spoon, preferably with a shallow bowl which is gentle on your baby's gums. Look out for packs of weaning spoons in chemists or baby-care shops. If you don't want to buy a lot of equipment straight away you may find it useful to mix small quantities of baby rice in the sterilized cap of a bottle. Alternatively, use a small china ramekin or plastic bowl. Plastic bowls with suction feet or keep-warm linings are also perfectly adequate and will be useful later on when baby gets bigger. All equipment must be sterilized first and water must be previously boiled and cooled before use.

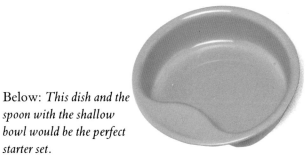

Below: *This dish and the spoon with the shallow bowl would be the perfect starter set.*

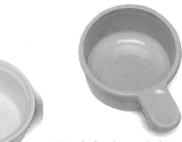

Top left, above, left and below: *Any small dish, or even the lid off a baby's bottle, can be used for mixing and feeding so long as it is thoroughly sterilized.*

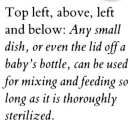

Below: *Bib*

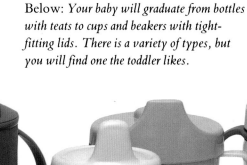

Left: *Bowl with keep-warm lining.*

Below: *Your baby will graduate from bottles with teats to cups and beakers with tight-fitting lids. There is a variety of types, but you will find one the toddler likes.*

FEEDING TWINS

Probably the easiest way is to sit each child in their car or baby seat, side by side and offer food from one bowl. Twins can get rather frustrated if you have to keep picking up different bowls and spoons. Try to be adaptable and if you find a way that works then stick with it. Encourage finger foods slightly earlier: perhaps a tiny ham sandwich, cooked broccoli floret or carrot stick.

Wait until each child has finished their main course before offering pudding as the slow eater will be distracted and want to go on to pudding too.

Looking after twins can be exhausting so you may find serving sandwiches for lunch an easier option and this will give you a chance to eat something too. Serve a cooked main meal for tea.

DRINKS

Although your baby will need less milk for nourishment, she will still need something to drink, especially in hot weather. Always offer at least two drinks during the day along with a drink with every meal.

You can give:

- milk – breast, formula milk or, at over one year, full-fat cows' milk
- cooled boiled water
- well-diluted pure unsweetened fruit juice.

Above: *Dilute juices with boiled water.*

You can stop boiling the water for baby's drinks when you stop sterilizing her feeding equipment, but always make sure you give water from the mains' supply and allow the tap to run before using. Never use water from the hot tap.

If you have a water softener make sure that you use a tap connected directly to the mains' supply and independent of the water softener. Artificially softened water is not recommended as salts are added during the softening process. Check with your health visitor before giving a baby bottled water as the mineral content varies and you will need to choose a low-mineral brand such as those labelled "spring water". As a general rule, bottled water is not really necessary unless you are holidaying somewhere where it is unsafe to drink the water.

Some fruit drinks contain a lot of added sugar, so check the label for sucrose, glucose, dextrose, fructose, maltose, syrup, honey or concentrated fruit juice. If you do give concentrated drinks to your baby make sure you dilute them correctly and do not give them too often. Pure fruit juices contain no

Above: *Feed twins side by side, alternating servings between the two.*

Below: *Drinks fill up the baby's tummy – so offer drinks* after *food.*

added sugar. At first, dilute them one part juice to three parts water. The amount of water can be reduced as the child matures. Offer drinks at the end of meal times once your baby is settled into three meals a day.

Never allow a baby to use a bottle of juice as a comforter or go to sleep with a bottle in his mouth as this can result in serious tooth decay.

Food Preparation

At this first stage it is vital that whatever solid food you offer should be smooth and soft in texture. Puréeing foods is very simple and there are plenty of gadgets available to make it even easier. For ease and speed, an electric liquidizer is by far the best. You may be able to buy a liquidizer attachment for your mixer or look out for a freestanding liquidizer unit. Prices vary considerably so it's worth shopping around. A food processor works well, but make sure the food is blended to a very fine purée before offering it to your baby, since processors can miss the odd lump, especially when processing small quantities. A hand-held electric multimixer is another useful gadget with the bonus of reducing washing up by mixing foods directly in the serving bowl. If you prefer to purée food by hand, then a sieve or hand mill are both perfectly adequate and are much cheaper alternatives.

Above: *There is a huge range of brand-name food processors and blenders on the market, many of which have attachments for puréeing.*

Left: *The basics – manual mashers, or a sieve – take longer but will do the job just as well.*

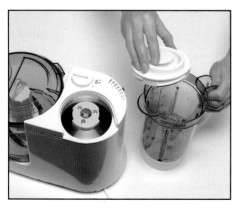

Above: *A purpose-designed liquidizer will make perfect purée in seconds. This is the right tool for making large batches.*

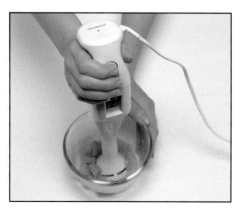

Above: *This hand-held blender takes a little longer, but the results are just as reliable. They are easy to clean and store.*

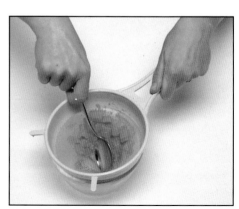

Above: *Making purée manually the old-fashioned way – with sieve and spoon – is time-consuming but highly satisfying.*

FOOD HYGIENE

Young babies can easily pick up infections so it is vitally important that all equipment is scrupulously clean before use.

● Always wash your hands before handling food or feeding equipment.

Above: *Rule one – always wash your hands before feeding your baby or handling food.*

● All items such as bottles, feeding spoons and serving bowls should be sterilized in the usual way, by boiling in a saucepan of water for 25 minutes, immersing in a container of cold water with sterilizing fluid or tablet, or by using a steam sterilizer. Larger items such as a sieve, knife, saucepan, blender or masher or plastic chopping board should be scalded with boiling water.

Above: *Scald larger objects with boiling water to sterilize.*

Right: *Always keep the surfaces around where your baby eats scrupulously clean.*

Above: *There is a wide range of sterilizing equipment to choose from. This group, all specially designed for bottles and teats, comprises two steam sterilizing units that operate electrically and a traditional container (see right) that holds the bottles efficiently in cold water sterilizing solution.*

SOLUTION STERILIZER

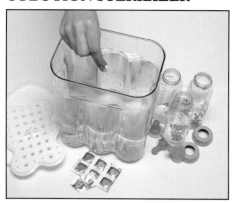

1 Fill the sterilizer to the required height with cold water, and add sterilizing tablets or liquid.

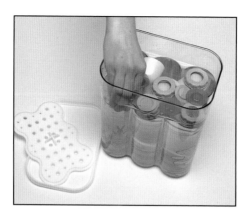

2 Pack the items to be sterilized into the container. Bottles will fit into the spaces provided.

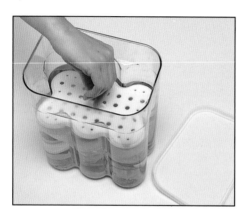

3 Make sure no air gets trapped in the container – or these pockets will not be properly sterile. Push everything down with the 'float'.

4 Place the lid on and leave for the length of time specified in the instructions. Rinse everything afterwards in boiling water.

STEAM STERILIZER

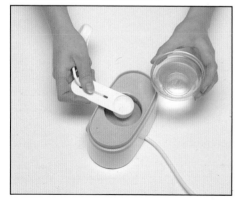

1 Measure the specified amount of water in to the base of the steamer as directed in the manufacturer's instructions.

2 Pack the bottles and teats in to the container: steamers have less capacity for dishes or jugs, which will need to be boiled separately.

- Sterilize all baby equipment until she is six months; milk bottles, teats etc. should be sterilized until she goes on to a cup.

Above: *Boiling in water for 25 minutes is still the simplest method of sterilizing.*

- Never use equipment used for the family pet when preparing baby food. Keep a tin opener, fork and dish specifically for your pet and make sure other members of the family are aware of this.
- Once cooked, cover all baby food with a lid or plate and transfer to the fridge as soon as possible. Food should not be left for longer than 1½ hours at room temperature before either refrigerating or freezing.

Above: *Always cover baby food at all times – even when stored in the refrigerator.*

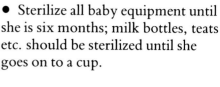
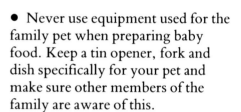

STERILIZING IN THE MICROWAVE

Microwave ovens are not suitable for general day-to-day sterilizing without special equipment, and many health authorities and mother and baby experts specifically recommend against using the microwave for this purpose.

However microwave sterilizing units can be purchased for sterilizing bottles, and where used, the manufacturer's instructions should be followed closely.

Right: This purpose-designed sterilizing unit is specially made for microwave use.

BATCH COOKING

Cooking for a tiny baby can be very frustrating. Those tiny spoonfuls of super-smooth purée so lovingly and hygienically prepared, offered with such hope and spat out so unceremoniously can leave you feeling quite indignant.

Save time by cooking several meals in advance. Freeze mini portions in ice-cube trays, great for those early days when you need only one cube for lunch and flexible enough for later weeks when your baby's appetite has grown to two or three cubes per meal.

Spoon the mixture into sterilized ice-cube trays and open freeze until solid. Press the cubes into a plastic bag, seal, label and return to the freezer. Keep batches of food in the same bag so flavours don't get muddled.

Recycle yogurt pots, cottage cheese pots with lids, small plastic boxes with lids or use disposable plastic cups and cover with clear film. Sterilize using sterilizing fluid or tablets. Cover all prepared foods and label clearly so you know what they are and when they went into the freezer.

Most foods should be used within three months if stored in a freezer at −18°C/0°F. Defrost plastic boxes in the fridge overnight. Ice cubes can be left to defrost at room temperature in a bowl or on a plate, loosely covered with clear film.

BATCH COOKING TIPS

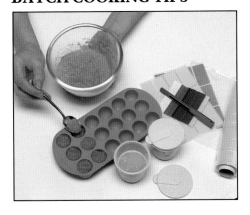

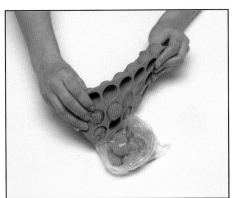

1 It is just as quick (and very much cheaper in the long run) to make a larger batch of purée as a smaller quantity for a single meal.

2 Freeze in meal-sized portions in sterilized ice-cube trays: these can later be turned out in to freezer bags for storing.

3 Make sure the bags are carefully labelled and dated. Keep only for the period specified in your freezer handbook.

STAGE 1: FIRST TASTES – AROUND FOUR MONTHS

THE FIRST SOLIDS ARE A STEPPING-STONE TO INTRODUCING YOUR BABY TO REAL FOOD SO SHE BECOMES FAMILIAR WITH ALL SORTS OF DIFFERENT TASTES AND TEXTURES.

ALTHOUGH MILK IS STILL PROVIDING YOUR BABY WITH ALL HER NUTRITIONAL NEEDS THESE EARLY FOODS WILL BE THE GROUNDS ON WHICH LATER EATING HABITS ARE BUILT, SO IT IS IMPORTANT THAT THIS IS A HAPPY, POSITIVE EXPERIENCE. IT IS IMPORTANT TO BUILD ON GOOD FOUNDATIONS.

BEGIN BY OFFERING ONLY A TEASPOONFUL OF VERY SOFT RUNNY PURÉE ONCE A DAY, GRADUALLY BUILDING TO 10–15 ML/2–3 TSP AND THEN SLOWLY ON TO TWO AND THREE MEALS A DAY.

Suitable Foods

FOODS TO INCLUDE
- baby rice mixed with water, breast or formula milk.
- mild-tasting vegetable purées – beginning with potato then going on to carrot, parsnip, or swede purée.
- mild, naturally-sweet fruit purées made with dessert apples or pears.

Apple

Pear

Swede

Carrot

Potato

Parsnip

Swede purée

Parsnip purée

Carrot purée

Potato purée

Pear purée

Dessert apple purée

Baby rice

FOODS TO AVOID
- highly spiced foods
- salt as this causes the kidneys to overwork. Avoid seasoning with salt or adding stock cubes, bacon and salami to foods
- cows' milk (give breast or formula milk feeds instead)
- foods containing gluten found in wheat, oats, rye and barley (check pack labels)
- eggs
- meat, fish, poultry
- citrus fruits – can result in allergic reactions in some babies
- nuts, either whole or ground
- honey
- fatty foods

Right: Adult favourites – but these must be avoided at this age, even as treats.

Note: If you have a family history of allergies, your doctor or health visitor may also advise you to avoid other foods. Do check with them.

Above: *A world of foodstuffs opens up over the months: but introduce them gradually, and at the right time.*

Baby Rice

Mix 5–15ml/1–3tsp rice with cooled boiled water, breast or formula milk as the pack directs. Cool slightly and test before serving.

Left: *Plain baby rice will be the staple for your baby for the first few weeks of solids – then gradually add flavour and variation.*

Vegetable Purées

Makes: 175ml/6fl oz/¾ cup

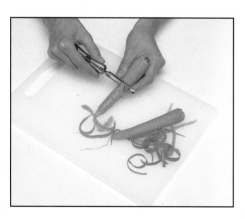

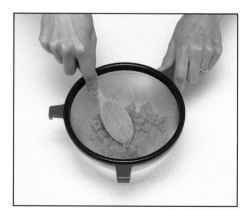

1 Peel 100g/4oz potato, parsnip, carrot or swede and dice.

2 Steam over a saucepan of boiling water for 10 minutes, until soft.

3 Press through a sieve, mix with 60–75ml/4–5tbsp formula or breast milk depending on the vegetable used. Spoon a little into a bowl, test on a spoon and cool if needed. Cover the remaining purée and transfer to the fridge as soon as possible. Use within 24 hours.

● To microwave, put the vegetable or vegetables in a microwave-proof bowl with 30ml/2tbsp formula or breast milk. Cover with clear film, pierce and cook on Full Power (100%) for 4 minutes. Leave to stand for 5 minutes, then press through a sieve and mix with 30–45ml/2–3tbsp formula or breast milk. Cool and serve as above.

Right: *This lovely selection of simple but satisfying vegetable purées illustrates that these bland foods need not lack colour and variation, and can be made very attractive to the infant.*

Fruit Purées

Makes: 120ml/4fl oz/½ cup

1 Peel, quarter and core 1 dessert apple or 1 ripe pear.

2 Thinly slice and put in a small saucepan with 15ml/1tbsp water, formula or breast milk. Cover and simmer for 10 minutes until soft.

● **To microwave:** place the apple or pear in a microwave-proof bowl with water, formula or breast milk. Cover with clear film, pierce and cook on Full Power (100%) for 3 minutes. Leave to stand for 5 minutes then press through a sieve. Cool and serve as above.

3 Press through a sieve. Spoon a little purée into a serving bowl, test on a spoon and cool if needed. Cover, transfer to the fridge, and use within 24 hours.

Top: *Pear (top) and apple purée will bring a smile to any baby's face (above).*

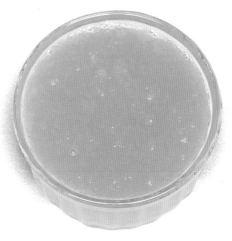

Melon purée

Strawberry purée

These tasty purées will encourage even reluctant eaters to take solids regularly.

Right: *When your baby is ready to start taking solids at around four to five months old, start with a teaspoon and build gradually to two and finally three meals a day.*

Warning: *Soft berry fruits should be introduced at around five to six months at the earliest. Do so in very small portions as some infants may have allergies and always sieve the purée carefully to remove berry pips.*

STAGE 2: AROUND FIVE TO SIX MONTHS

B Y NOW YOUR BABY MAY BE TAKING SOLIDS AT TWO OR THREE MEALS EACH DAY. INCREASE THE VARIETY OF FOODS OFFERED AND START TO COMBINE FOOD TASTES. BABY PURÉE CAN BE A SLIGHTLY THICKER COARSER TEXTURE, BUT MAKE SURE THERE ARE NO PIPS OR BONES. ALWAYS CHOOSE THE BEST, FRESHEST INGREDIENTS AND MAKE SURE UTENSILS ARE SCRUPULOUSLY CLEAN.

Suitable Foods

FOODS TO INCLUDE

- wider selection of vegetables including fresh or frozen peas, sweetcorn, cauliflower, broccoli, cabbage, spinach, celery, mushrooms, leeks
- poultry
- mild tasting fresh or frozen fish – plaice, cod, haddock, trout
- small quantities of very lean red meat
- small quantities of split pulses – peas, red lentils and very well cooked or canned whole pulses – chick-peas, beans
- more interesting fruits – banana, apricots, peaches, plums, strawberries, raspberries, melon (Warning: offer tiny amounts of soft berry fruits as some children may be allergic to them.)
- gluten-free cereals – rice, cornflour
- small quantities of cocoa

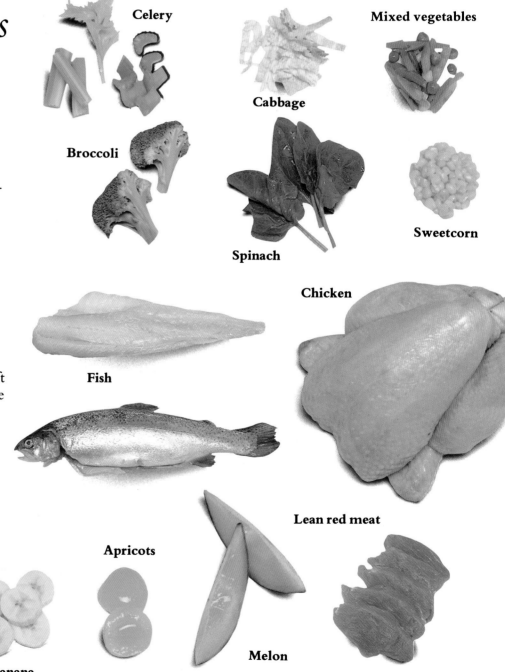

Celery

Mixed vegetables

Cabbage

Broccoli

Spinach

Sweetcorn

Chicken

Fish

Lean red meat

Plums

Banana

Apricots

Melon

Above: *Every day brings a new taste: these young gourmets can't wait!*

Chick-peas

Cocoa

Split peas

Cornflour

Lentils

Rice

FOODS TO AVOID

- gluten-based cereals, wheat flour and bread
- cows' milk and milk products
- eggs
- citrus fruit
- nuts, ground or whole
- fatty foods
- chillies and highly spiced foods

Below: *Even super-healthy adult foods such as wholewheat bread and oranges should still be avoided at this stage.*

Reheating, Freezing and Using a Microwave

REHEATING BABY FOOD

Reheating food sounds straightforward but it is vitally important that these rules are followed as tepid food provides the perfect breeding ground for bacteria, especially if left uncovered in a warm kitchen and reheated several times.

- Don't reheat food more than once. It is a health risk, and can be dangerous.

- If you have a large batch of baby food then reheat just a portion in a saucepan and leave the remaining mixture in a covered bowl in the fridge. If your baby is still hungry then reheat a little extra again with the remaining mixture left in the fridge.

- Reheat small quantities of baby food in a sterilized heat-proof container, covered with a saucer or small plate and put into a small saucepan half filled with boiling water. Or spoon larger quantities straight into a saucepan, cover and bring to the boil.

- Make sure food is piping hot all the way through to kill any bacteria. Food should be 70°C/158°F for a minimum of 2 minutes. Take off the heat and allow to cool. Test before serving to baby.

REHEATING TIPS

1 Reheat small quantities in a sterilized bowl, covered with a dish or silver foil.

2 Place the bowl into a pan half filled with boiling water. Make sure the food is cooked through.

3 For larger quantities, put the food straight into the pan and bring to the boil.

FREEZING

When using a freezer for storing homemade baby foods, use up the foods as soon as possible as the texture preferred by the child will change very quickly as the child develops.

Keeping a well-stocked freezer of basic stores can be a lifesaver: there is nothing worse than going shopping with little children, especially when they're tired and freezing will save you trip after trip.

Make sure to always label foods so you know exactly when they went into the freezer and double check against this handy list of storage dates:

Meat and poultry

Beef and lamb	4–6 months
Pork and veal	4–6 months
Minced beef	3–4 months
Sausages and sausagemeat	2–3 months
Ham and bacon joints	3–4 months
Chicken and turkey	10–12 months
Duck and goose	4–6 months

Fish

White fish	6–8 months
Oily fish	3–4 months
Fish portions	3–4 months
Shellfish	2–3 months

Fruit and vegetables

Fruit with or without sugar	8–10 months
Fruit juices	4–6 months
Most vegetables	10–12 months
Mushrooms and tomatoes	6–8 months

Dairy produce

Cream	6–8 months
Butter, unsalted	6–8 months
Butter, salted	3–4 months
Cheese, hard	4–6 months
Cheese, soft	3–4 months
Ice cream	3–4 months

Prepared foods

Ready prepared meals, highly seasoned	2–3 months
Ready prepared meals, average seasoning	4–6 months
Cakes	4–6 months
Bread, all kinds	2–3 months
Other yeast products and pastries	3–4 months

* Chart published by kind permission of the Food Safety Advisory Centre

USING A MICROWAVE

Health advisers do not recommend using a microwave for reheating as the food heats up unevenly but if you decide to microwave baby food then make sure you stir the food thoroughly after cooking. Leave the dish to stand for 2–3 minutes before stirring again so that "hot spots" are well stirred into the mixture, and always check the temperature before serving. Choose the type of dish carefully as some pottery dishes can get very hot; plastic or pyrex dishes are the most successful in the microwave, heating food quickly but staying relatively cool themselves.

Top: *All parents will find the microwave incredibly helpful and time-saving. It can be used for heating milk and drinks (for toddlers – not newborns), for defrosting, reheating and cooking preprepared foods.*

1 Cover the dish with clear film, pierce and place in the oven.

2 When cooked, remove and stir.

MICROWAVING TIPS

● Never warm milk for a new born or young baby in the microwave.

● For older children warm milk in a bottle without the teet or an uncovered feeder beaker for 30–45 seconds. Stir well and always test the temperature of the milk (*not* the temperature of the container) before serving to make sure that the milk is an even and comfortable temperature. Do also seek advice from your health visitor.

● To defrost ice cubes of baby food, press three into a baby dish, cover with clear film and thaw in the microwave on Defrost (30%) setting for 1 to 2 minutes. Stir well then re-cover and microwave on Full Power (100%) for 1 minute. Stir well to avoid hot spots then test the temperature.

Autumn Harvest

Makes: 600ml/1 pint/2½ cups

115g/4oz carrot
115g/4oz parsnip
115g/4oz swede
115g/4oz potato
300ml/½ pint/1¼ cups formula milk

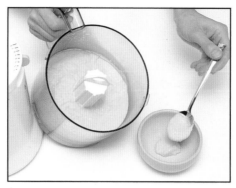

4 Spoon a little into a bowl. Test the temperature and cool if necessary, before giving to baby.

5 Cover the remaining food and transfer to the fridge as soon as possible. Use within 24 hours.

- Suitable for freezing.

TIP
Thin the purée down with a little extra formula milk if your baby prefers a very soft purée.

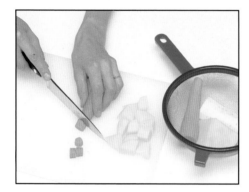

1 Trim and peel the carrot, parsnip, swede and potato and place in a colander. Rinse under cold water, drain and chop.

2 Place the chopped vegetables in a saucepan with the formula milk then bring to the boil, cover and simmer for 20 minutes or until they are very soft.

3 Purée or sieve the vegetables until they are smooth.

Mixed Vegetable Platter

Makes: 600ml/1 pint/2½ cups

115g/4oz carrot

175g/6oz potato

115g/4oz broccoli

50g/2oz green cabbage

300ml/½ pint/1¼ cups formula milk

1 Peel the carrot and potato, rinse, chop and place in a saucepan. Wash the broccoli and cabbage and cut the broccoli into florets, the stems into slices and shred the cabbage finely.

2 Add the milk to the carrot and potato, bring to the boil then cover and simmer for 10 minutes.

3 Add the broccoli stems and florets and cabbage and cook, covered, for 10 minutes until all the vegetables are tender.

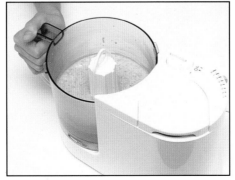

4 Purée or sieve the vegetables until smooth.

5 Spoon a little into a bowl. Test the temperature and cool if necessary, before giving to baby.

6 Cover the remaining food and transfer to the fridge as soon as possible. Use within 24 hours.

● Suitable for freezing.

Carrot, Lentil and Coriander Purée

Makes: 600ml/1 pint/2½ cups

350g/12oz carrots
175g/6oz potato
50g/2oz/¼ cup red lentils
2.5ml/½ tsp ground coriander
300ml/½ pint/1¼ cups formula milk

1 Trim and peel the carrots and potatoes and then chop into small cubes and place in a saucepan. Rinse the lentils thoroughly, discarding any black bits.

2 Add the lentils, coriander and milk to the pan and bring to the boil, then cover and simmer for 40 minutes, until the lentils are very soft. Top up with a little extra boiling water if necessary.

TIP
The mixture thickens on cooling so any remaining mixture will need to be thinned slightly with a little formula milk before reheating for the next meal.

3 Purée or sieve the vegetable and lentil mixture until smooth.

4 Spoon a little into a bowl. Test the temperature and cool if necessary, before giving to baby.

5 Cover the remaining purée and transfer to the fridge as soon as possible. Use within 24 hours.

• Suitable for freezing.

Red Pepper Risotto

Makes: 600ml/1 pint/2½ cups

50g/2oz/¼ cup long grain rice

300ml/½ pint/1¼ cups formula milk

75g/3oz red pepper

75g/3oz courgette

50g/2oz celery

1 Place the rice and milk in a saucepan, bring to the boil and simmer, uncovered, for 5 minutes.

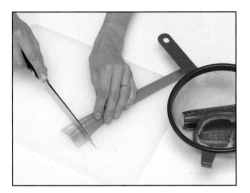

2 Discard the core and seeds from the pepper and trim the courgette and celery. Place the vegetables in a colander and rinse under cold water then chop them into small pieces.

3 Add the vegetables to the rice mixture, bring to the boil, cover and simmer for about 10 minutes or until the rice is soft.

● Suitable for freezing.

4 Purée or sieve the rice and vegetable mixture until smooth.

5 Spoon a little into a bowl. Test the temperature and cool if necessary, before giving to baby.

6 Cover the remaining food and transfer to the fridge as soon as possible. Use within 24 hours.

Parsnip and Broccoli Mix

Makes: 600ml/1 pint/2½ cups

225g/8oz parsnips

115g/4oz broccoli

300ml/½ pint/1¼ cups formula milk

1 Trim and peel the parsnips and place in a colander with the broccoli. Rinse the parsnips and broccoli under cold water. Chop the parsnips and cut the broccoli into florets, slicing the stems.

2 Put the parsnips in a saucepan with the milk, bring to the boil, then cover and simmer for about 10 minutes.

3 Add the broccoli and simmer for a further 10 minutes, until the vegetables are soft.

4 Purée or sieve the vegetable mixture to make a completely smooth purée.

5 Spoon a little into a bowl. Test the temperature and cool if necessary, before giving to baby.

6 Cover the remaining purée and transfer to the fridge as soon as possible. Use within 24 hours.

● Suitable for freezing.

Turkey Stew with Carrots and Sweetcorn

Makes: 600ml/1 pint/2½ cups

175g/6oz potato

175g/6oz carrot

115g/4oz turkey breast, skinned and boned

50g/2oz/⅓ cup frozen sweetcorn

300ml/½ pint/1¼ cups formula milk

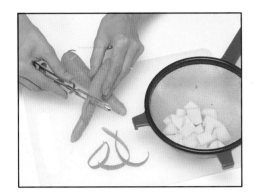

1 Trim and peel the potato and carrots, rinse under cold water and then chop into small cubes.

2 Rinse the turkey and cut into thin strips. Place in a small saucepan with the potato and carrot.

TIP
Bring the mixture to the boil in a flameproof casserole and transfer to a preheated oven 180°C/350°F/ Gas 4 and cook for 1¼ hours if preferred.

3 Add the sweetcorn and milk. Cover and simmer for 20 minutes, until the turkey is cooked. Purée or sieve the mixture until completely smooth.

4 Spoon a little into a bowl. Test the temperature and cool if necessary, before giving to baby.

5 Cover the remaining food and refrigerate. Use within 24 hours.

- Suitable for freezing.

Chicken and Parsnip Purée

Makes: 600ml/1 pint/2½ cups

350g/12oz parsnips

115g/4oz chicken breast, skinned and boned

300ml/½ pint/1¼ cups formula milk

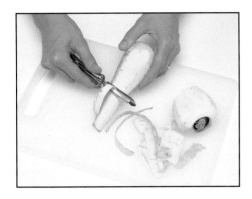

1 Peel the parsnips, and trim the woody tops and bottoms. Rinse and chop roughly.

2 Rinse the chicken under cold water and cut into small pieces.

3 Place the parsnips, chicken and milk in a saucepan. Cover and simmer for 20 minutes or until the parsnips are tender.

4 Purée or sieve the chicken and parsnip mixture until smooth.

5 Spoon into a bowl. Test the temperature and cool if necessary, before giving to baby.

6 Cover the remaining purée and transfer to the fridge as soon as possible. Use within 24 hours.

• Suitable for freezing.

TIP
For a very smooth purée, drain all the liquid into a liquidizer and add half the solids, blend until smooth then add the remaining ingredients. If using a food processor, add all the solids and a little liquid, process until smooth then add the remaining liquid.

Cock-a-Leekie Casserole

Makes: 600ml/1 pint/2½ cups

50g/2oz leek

275g/10oz potatoes

115g/4oz chicken breast, skinned
and boned

300ml/½ pint/1¼ cups formula milk

1 Halve the leek lengthways and
rinse under running water to
remove any dirt or grit.

2 Peel potatoes and cut into small
dice. Rinse the chicken and cut
into pieces and thinly slice the leek.

3 Place the vegetables and chicken
in a saucepan with the milk.

4 Bring the mixture to the boil,
cover with a lid and simmer
gently for 20 minutes, until the
potatoes are just tender. Purée or
sieve the mixture until it is
completely smooth.

5 Spoon a little into a bowl. Test
the temperature and cool if
necessary, before giving to baby.
Use within 24 hours.

● Suitable for freezing.

TIP
You can vary the texture of this
recipe depending on how you
purée the mixture. A fine sieve
produces the finest consistency,
then a food processor, while a food
mill gives the coarsest texture.
Starchy vegetables thicken and
bind the purée together. Any root
vegetable can be used for this
recipe, but make sure it is
thoroughly cooked before blending.

Trout and Courgette Savoury

Makes: 600ml/1 pint/2½ cups

| 275g/10oz potatoes |
| 175g/6oz courgettes |
| 115g/4oz pink trout fillet |
| 250ml/8fl oz/1 cup formula milk |

1 Peel the potatoes, trim the courgettes and rinse under cold water. Dice the potatoes and cut the courgettes into slices.

2 Place the vegetables in a saucepan. Rinse the trout and arrange on top, then pour over the milk. Bring to the boil, cover and simmer for 15 minutes, until the potatoes and fish are cooked.

3 Lift the trout out of the pan and peel off the skin. Break it into pieces with a knife and fork, checking carefully for any bones.

4 Purée or sieve the fish, the vegetables and the liquid until quite smooth.

5 Spoon a little into a bowl. Test the temperature and cool if necessary, before giving to baby.

6 Cover any remaining food and transfer to the fridge as soon as possible. Use within 24 hours.

● Suitable for freezing.

Fisherman's Pie

Makes: 600ml/1 pint/2½ cups

350g/12oz potatoes
90g/3½oz brick frozen skinless cod
25g/1oz/¼ cup frozen peas
25g/1oz/2 tbsp frozen sweetcorn
300ml/½ pint/1¼ cups formula milk

1 Peel and rinse the potatoes and cut into even-sized pieces. Place in a saucepan with the fish, peas, sweetcorn and milk.

2 Bring to the boil, cover and simmer for 15 minutes until the potatoes are very tender.

3 Lift the fish out of the pan and break into pieces with a knife and fork, checking carefully and removing any small bones.

4 Purée or sieve fish, vegetables and cooking liquid until completely smooth.

5 Spoon a little into a bowl. Test the temperature and cool if necessary, before giving to baby.

6 Cover the remaining purée and place in the fridge as soon as possible. Use within 24 hours.

- Suitable for freezing.

Apple Ambrosia

Makes: 300ml/½ pint/1¼ cups

1 dessert apple

25g/1oz flaked rice

300ml/½ pint/1¼ cups formula milk

1 Quarter, core and peel the apple. Slice thinly and place in a saucepan with the rice and milk.

2 Bring to the boil then simmer over a gentle heat for 10–12 minutes until the rice is soft, stirring occasionally with a wooden spoon.

3 Purée the apple and rice mixture until completely smooth.

4 Spoon into a bowl. Test the temperature and cool if necessary, before giving to baby. Cover the remaining purée and transfer to the fridge as soon as possible. Use within 24 hours.

VARIATION
Chocolate Pudding

Cook the rice as above but without the apple. Stir 25g/1oz milk chocolate dots and 15ml/1tbsp caster sugar into the hot rice and then purée until smooth. Spoon into small dishes and cool as necessary.

Fruit Salad Purée

Makes: 350ml/12fl oz/1½ cups

1 nectarine or peach
1 dessert apple
1 ripe pear
25g/1oz fresh or frozen raspberries or strawberries

1 Halve the nectarine or peach, discard the stone then peel and chop. Peel, quarter and core the apple and pear and slice thinly.

2 Put the prepared fruits, the hulled raspberries or strawberries and 15ml/1 tbsp water in a saucepan. Cover and simmer for 10 minutes until the fruit is soft.

3 Press the mixture through a sieve or process and then sieve to remove the berry pips. Discard the pips.

4 Spoon a little into a baby bowl. Test the temperature and cool if necessary, before giving to baby.

5 Cover the remaining purée and transfer to the fridge as soon as possible. Use within 24 hours.

● Suitable for freezing.

TIP
Babies tend to eat smaller quantities of dessert so it is best to open freeze purée in a sterilized ice cube tray. Transfer the cubes to a plastic bag once frozen.

VARIATION
Peach and Melon Blush
To make 175ml/6 fl oz/¾ cup, take 1 ripe peach and ¼ ripe charentais melon. Peel and halve the peach, discard the stone and cut up the fruit. Scoop the seeds out of the melon and cut away the skin. Roughly chop the melon into pieces.
   Purée or sieve the fruit until completely smooth. Spoon a little into a bowl and serve.

STAGE 3: SIX TO NINE MONTHS

Baby purée can be processed or mashed but still needs to be fairly soft. A few small bits can be introduced, but be guided by your baby and adjust the textures as required. As always, don't rush things and go at your baby's pace.

If liked, let your baby hold a second spoon while you are feeding her to help develop co-ordination. This is the first step towards self-feeding.

All the recipes from the previous section can still be made for your growing baby; just adjust the texture so that foods are slightly coarser.

Suitable Foods

FOODS TO INCLUDE
- wheat-based foods, pasta, bread – first fingers of toast or bread sticks
- breakfast cereals such as Ready Brek or Weetabix made up with cows' milk
- cows' milk and dairy foods, e.g. yogurt, cottage cheese, mild Cheddar and Edam cheese
- red meat, but make sure you trim off fat and gristle
- hard-boiled egg yolk
- citrus fruits
- fingers of cooked carrot, broccoli
- smooth peanut butter

Breakfast cereals

Mild cheeses

Yogurt

Lean red meat

Cottage cheese

Bread

Fish

Pasta

Citrus fruit

Cooked egg yolk

Peanut butter

Broccoli and carrot

Above: *At six to nine months your baby will be delighted to try pasta and cheese.*

FOODS TO AVOID
- egg white
- whole or chopped nuts
- canned fish in brine
- organ meats – liver, kidney
- chillies and other very spicy foods
- salty foods
- sugary foods

Right: *There is still a wide range of fatty, salty and spicy foods that must be avoided.*

Choosing a Highchair

There is a surprisingly wide choice of highchairs available in a range of finishes, colours and price levels so make sure you shop around before you buy.

CONVERTIBLE CHAIRS

Designed for babies between four weeks and six months, these chairs can convert from a highchair into a swing and some models into a baby chair and rocker too. It is best to buy one of these when the baby is very young so that you get maximum use from it. The only disadvantage may be the space required for the frame. The ease in converting from one type of chair to another varies from model to model, so you would be well advised to practise in the shop before buying. Most chairs have white painted frames.

THREE-IN-ONE CHAIRS

Various designs on the market convert into a separate chair, chair and table or highchair. Some simply clip apart while others require a little help with a screwdriver. There are good rigid structures available with a wide range of decorative seat patterns. They are available in wood or white finishes. The low chair is suitable for children up to four years old if used without the tray.

ELEVATOR CHAIRS

These slightly more expensive chairs convert from a highchair to a low chair. Some models have adjustable tray settings to fit a growing child. The frames are mostly available in white metal, with attractive seating.

Three-in-one type

Elevator type

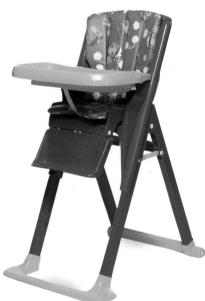

TIPS
- For maximum use of a highchair, buy a booster cushion for the early days when your baby first begins to use the chair. Adjust the tray position as well, if possible.
- Check that the highchair is easy to clean – dried-on rusk can be impossible to clean off. Look out for possible dirt traps on the seat or around the tray fixing.
- Make sure that the chair is sturdy and rigid – it will need to withstand considerable wear.

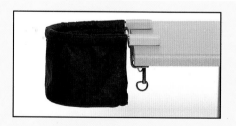

Above: *A portable clip-on chair.*

- If using a clip-on highchair make sure that the table is suitable and will be able to withstand the weight of your child. Never, in any circumstances, fix on to glass.

FOLDING CHAIRS

These less expensive chairs, available in wood or white finishes, usually fold up in a scissor movement. Some can be folded crossways for packing into the boot of the car. Before buying, check how easy they are to fold out and up and make sure the frame is rigid when opened out.

Folding type

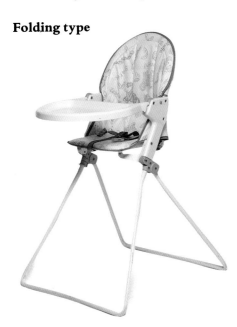

COUNTRY-TYPE CHAIRS

These are sturdy wooden highchairs usually with a wooden tray and attractive cottage-style spindle features. The seat can be hard for baby so it is best to buy a fitted chair cushion.

PORTABLE CHAIRS

There are two main types available:
● a very simple cloth tie, useful for visiting friends or eating out as it will fold up and fit in a bag. However, it is not really suitable for everyday use as the child is literally tied on to the chair and so cannot reach the table to feed himself.
● clip-on seats where the frames are placed under and over the edge of a dining table. Check that the table is strong enough and is not likely to overbalance before you put your baby in the chair.

1 Undo the tray catches by pressing both sides at once, and fold the tray upwards.

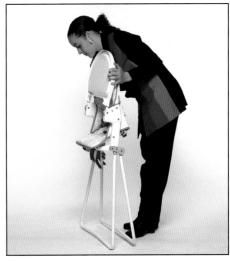

2 Undo the side catches which keep the frame rigid so the chair can scissor in two.

3 This allows you to fold the chair over on to itself: the design is incredibly neat and compact.

4 It is now ready for storing, putting out of the way, or popping in to the boot of the car.

TIPS
● Always use a safety harness. Although most highchairs have a three point lap strap you will probably have to buy straps that will go around your baby's body and clip on to the chair. It is amazing how quickly a baby learns to wriggle out of a highchair when you're not looking.
● Never leave a child in a highchair unattended.

Above: *Always strap your baby in tightly.*

Shepherd's Pie

Makes: 600ml/1 pint/2½ cups

2 tomatoes
¼ onion
225g/8oz potato
50g/2oz button mushrooms
115g/4oz lean minced beef
250ml/8fl oz/1 cup water
15ml/1 tbsp tomato ketchup
pinch of dried mixed herbs

1 Make a cross cut in each tomato, put in a small bowl and cover with boiling water. Leave to stand for 1 minute and then drain and peel off the skins. Cut into quarters and scoop out the seeds.

2 Finely chop the onion, chop the potato and slice the mushrooms.

3 Dry-fry the beef in a saucepan for 5 minutes, stirring until browned all over.

• Suitable for freezing.

4 Add the tomatoes, potato, mushrooms and onion and cook for a further 3 minutes. Stir well to blend all the flavours together.

5 Add the water, ketchup and herbs. Bring to the boil then reduce the heat, cover and simmer for 40 minutes until the meat and vegetables are tender.

6 Process or mash the meat and vegetables just enough to give the desired consistency.

7 Spoon a little into a bowl. Test the temperature and cool if necessary, before giving to baby.

8 Cover the remainder and refrigerate. Use within 24 hours.

Braised Beef and Carrots

Makes: 600ml/1 pint/2½ cups

175g/6oz potato
225g/8oz carrots
¼ onion
175g/6oz stewing beef
300ml/½ pint/1¼ cups water
pinch of dried mixed herbs

1 Preheat the oven to 180°C/ 350°F/Gas 4. Peel and chop the potato, carrots and onion and place in a flameproof casserole.

2 Rinse the beef, cut away any fat and gristle and cut into small cubes using a sharp knife.

3 Add the meat, water and herbs to the casserole, bring to the boil and then cover and cook in the oven for 1½ hours or until the meat is tender and the vegetables are soft.

4 Process or mash the ingredients to the desired consistency and spoon a little into a bowl. Test the temperature and cool if necessary, before giving to baby.

5 Cover any unused food and transfer to the fridge as soon as possible. Use within 24 hours.

● Suitable for freezing.

TIP
Replace the carrots with any other root vegetable such as parsnip or swede, if wished.

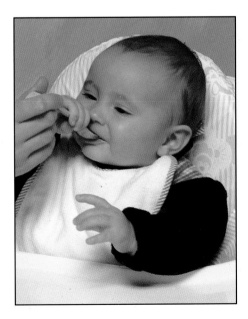

Lamb Hotpot

Makes: 600ml/1 pint/2½ cups

115g/4oz potato
115g/4oz carrot
115g/4oz swede
50g/2oz leek
115g/4oz lamb fillet
300ml/½ pint/1¼ cup water
pinch of dried rosemary

1 Peel the potato, carrot and swede, rinse and chop into small cubes. Halve the leek lengthways, rinse well and slice. Place all the vegetables in a saucepan.

2 Rinse the lamb under cold water and chop into small pieces, discarding any fat.

3 Add the meat to the pan with the water and rosemary. Bring to the boil, cover and simmer for 30 minutes or until the lamb is thoroughly cooked.

4 Process or mash the ingredients to the desired consistency.

5 Spoon a little into a bowl, test the temperature and cool if necessary, before giving to baby.

6 Cover the remaining food and transfer to the fridge as soon as possible. Use within 24 hours.

• Suitable for freezing.

Lamb and Lentil Savoury

Makes: 600ml/1 pint/2½ cups

115g/4oz lamb fillet

115g/4oz swede

1 celery stick

25g/1oz/2 tbsp red lentils

15ml/1 tbsp tomato ketchup

350ml/12fl oz/1½ cups water

1 Rinse the lamb under cold water, trim off any fat and chop into small pieces. Peel the swede, place in a colander with the celery and rinse with cold water. Chop into cubes and place in a saucepan.

2 Put the lentils in a sieve and rinse under cold water, picking out any black bits. Add to the pan with the lamb and ketchup.

3 Add the water and bring to the boil, then cover and simmer for 40 minutes or until the lentils are soft. Top up with extra water during cooking if necessary, then process or mash just enough to give the desired consistency.

4 Spoon a little into a bowl, test the temperature and cool if necessary, before giving to baby.

5 Cover the remaining food and transfer to the fridge as soon as possible. Use within 24 hours.

● Suitable for freezing.

VARIATION
Substitute green lentils or split peas for the red lentils and a small courgette for the celery stick.

Country Pork and Green Beans

Makes: 450ml/¾ pint/1⅞ cups

115g/4oz lean pork

115g/4oz potato

115g/4oz carrot

75g/3oz runner beans

pinch of dried sage

350ml/12fl oz/1½ cups water

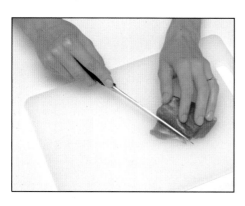

1 Rinse the pork under cold water, trim away any fat and gristle and chop into small cubes.

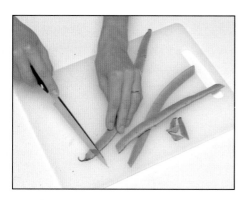

2 Peel the potato and carrot, trim the beans, rinse and chop.

3 Put the pork, potato and carrot in a saucepan with the sage and water. Bring to the boil, cover and simmer for 30 minutes.

4 Add the beans and cook, covered, for a further 10 minutes until all the vegetables are tender.

5 Process or mash to the desired consistency, then spoon a little into a bowl. Test the temperature before giving to baby.

6 Cover and transfer the remaining food to the fridge. Use within 24 hours.

● Suitable for freezing.

VARIATION

Instead of the pork, use any lean meat in this recipe, such as chicken or turkey. Add broad beans, with the outer skin removed, in place of the runner beans.

TIP
If runner beans are unavailable use French beans, sugar snap peas or broccoli. Look out for ready prepared diced pork in the supermarket. Cut into smaller pieces and make sure to remove any gristle before cooking.

Pork and Apple Savoury

Makes: 600ml/1 pint/2½ cups

175g/6oz lean pork

175g/6oz potato

175g/6oz swede or parsnip

¼ onion

½ dessert apple

300ml/½ pint/1¼ cups water

pinch of dried sage

1 Preheat the oven to 180°C/ 350°F/Gas 4. Rinse the pork under cold water, trim away any fat and gristle then chop. Peel and chop the vegetables. Peel, core and chop the apple.

2 Put the meat, vegetables, apple, water and sage in a flameproof casserole, cover and bring to the boil stirring once or twice.

3 Cover and cook in the oven for 1¼ hours until the meat is tender, then process or mash to the desired consistency.

4 Spoon a little into a bowl, test the temperature and cool if necessary, before giving to baby.

5 Cover the remaining food and transfer to the fridge as soon as possible. Use within 24 hours.

● Suitable for freezing.

TIP
The mixture can be cooked in a saucepan on the hob for 40 minutes if preferred.

Nursery Kedgeree

Makes: 600ml/1 pint/2½ cups

50g/2oz/¼ cup long grain rice

25g/1oz/2 tbsp frozen peas

350ml/12fl oz/1½ cups formula milk

90g/3¼oz brick frozen skinless cod

2 hard-boiled egg yolks

1 Place the rice, peas, milk and fish in a saucepan, bring to the boil, cover and simmer for 15 minutes, until the fish is cooked and the rice is soft.

2 Lift the fish out of the pan and break into pieces with a knife and fork, checking for bones.

3 Stir the fish into the rice mixture and add the egg yolks.

4 Mash with a fork to the desired consistency. Alternatively blend in a food processor, liquidizer or press through a sieve.

5 Spoon a little into a bowl, test the temperature and cool if necessary, before giving to baby.

6 Cover the remaining kedgeree and transfer to the fridge as soon as possible. Use within 24 hours.

TIP
Peas can be quite difficult to mash down. Check before giving to baby as whole peas are difficult for baby to chew.

- Suitable for freezing.

Mediterranean Vegetables

Makes: 600ml/1 pint/2½ cups

3 tomatoes

175g/6oz courgette

75g/3oz button mushrooms

115g/4oz red pepper

20ml/4 tsp tomato ketchup

250ml/8fl oz/1 cup water

pinch of dried mixed herbs

40g/1½oz dried pasta shapes

3 Rinse and slice the courgette and mushrooms. Chop the pepper.

4 Put the vegetables in a saucepan with the ketchup, water and herbs. Cover and simmer for 10 minutes or until tender.

5 Meanwhile cook the pasta in boiling water for 8–10 minutes until tender. Drain.

6 Mix the vegetables and pasta together and process or mash.

7 Spoon a little into a bowl, test the temperature and cool if necessary, before giving to baby.

8 Cover remaining mixture and refrigerate. Use within 24 hours.

● Suitable for freezing.

1 Make a cross cut in each tomato, put in a small bowl and cover with boiling water. Leave for 1 minute then drain and peel off the skins. Cut into quarters and scoop out the seeds from the tomatoes.

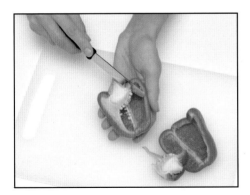

2 Trim the courgette and mushrooms and cut away the core and seeds from the pepper.

TIP
For adventurous eaters add ½ clove crushed garlic at Step 3.

Saucy Pasta

Makes: 600ml/1 pint/2½ cups

115g/4oz carrot

50g/2oz Brussels sprouts

25g/1oz green beans

25g/1oz/2 tbsp frozen sweetcorn

50g/2oz dried pasta shapes

350ml/12fl oz/1½ cups formula milk

50g/2oz mild Cheddar cheese

1 Peel the carrot, discard any discoloured outer leaves from the sprouts and trim the beans. Rinse and then chop into pieces.

2 Place the vegetables, sweetcorn, pasta and milk in a saucepan, bring to the boil and then simmer, uncovered, for 12–15 minutes until the pasta is cooked.

TIP
Vary the vegetables depending on what you have in the fridge.

3 Grate the cheese and add to the vegetables, stirring until the cheese has completely melted.

4 Process or mash just enough to give the desired consistency, then spoon a little into a bowl. Test the temperature and cool if necessary, before giving to baby.

5 Cover the remaining food and transfer to the fridge as soon as possible. Use within 24 hours.

● Suitable for freezing.

Apple and Orange Fool

Makes: 250ml/8fl oz/1 cup

2 dessert apples
5ml/1 tsp grated orange rind and 15ml/1 tbsp orange juice
15ml/1 tbsp custard powder
5ml/1 tsp caster sugar
150ml/¼ pint/⅔ cup formula milk

1 Quarter, core and peel the apples. Slice and place the apples in a saucepan with the orange rind and juice.

2 Cover and cook gently for 10 minutes, stirring occasionally until the apples are soft.

3 Blend the custard powder and sugar with a little of the milk to make a smooth paste. Bring the remaining milk to the boil and stir into the custard mixture.

4 Return the custard to the pan and slowly bring to the boil, stirring until thickened and smooth.

5 Process or mash the apple to the desired consistency. Add the custard and stir to mix.

6 Spoon a little into a bowl, test the temperature and cool if necessary, before giving to baby.

7 Cover the remaining fool and transfer to the fridge as soon as possible. Use within 24 hours.

• Suitable for freezing.

Orchard Fruit Dessert

Makes: 450ml/¾ pint/1⅞ cups

1 ripe pear
225g/8oz ripe plums
15ml/1 tbsp caster sugar
15ml/1 tbsp custard powder
150ml/¼ pint/⅔ cup formula milk

1 Quarter, core, peel and slice the pear. Wash the plums, then cut in half, stone and slice.

2 Put the fruit in a saucepan with 15ml/1 tbsp water and 10ml/ 2 tsp of the sugar. Cover and cook gently for 10 minutes until soft.

3 Blend the custard powder, remaining sugar and a little of the milk to a smooth paste.

4 Bring the remaining milk to the boil and gradually stir into the custard mixture. Pour the custard back into the pan and bring to the boil, stirring, until it is both thickened and smooth.

5 Process or mash the fruit to the desired consistency and stir in the custard. Spoon a little into a bowl, test the temperature and cool if necessary, before giving to baby.

6 Cover the remaining custard and transfer to the fridge as soon as possible. Use within 24 hours.

● Suitable for freezing.

Peach Melba Dessert

Makes: 175ml/6fl oz/¾ cup

1 ripe peach

25g/1oz fresh or frozen raspberries

15ml/1 tbsp icing sugar

115g/4oz natural Greek yogurt

1 Halve the peach, discard the stone then peel and slice. Place in a saucepan with the raspberries and 15ml/1 tbsp water.

2 Cover and cook gently for 10 minutes until soft.

3 Purée and press through a sieve to remove the raspberry pips.

4 Set aside to cool then stir in the sugar and swirl in the yogurt. Spoon a little into a baby dish.

5 Cover the remaining dessert and transfer to the fridge. Use within 24 hours.

VARIATION
Bananarama
To make a single portion, use ½ a small banana and 15ml/1 tbsp of natural Greek yogurt. Mash the banana until smooth and add the yogurt. Stir to mix and serve immediately. Do not make this dessert in advance, as the banana will discolour while standing.

TIP
The finished pudding is not suitable for freezing although the sweetened fruit purée can be frozen successfully in sections of an ice cube tray. Defrost cubes of purée and mix each cube with 15ml/ 1 tbsp yogurt.

STAGE 4: NINE TO TWELVE MONTHS

GRADUALLY PROGRESS FROM MINCED TO CHOPPED OR ROUGHLY MASHED FOOD. BY NOW YOUR BABY WILL BE ABLE TO JOIN IN WITH FAMILY MEALS AND EAT A LITTLE OF WHAT YOU ARE EATING. ENSURE THAT YOUR BABY IS EATING THREE MAIN MEALS AND TWO TO THREE SNACK MEALS PER DAY. YOUNG CHILDREN DEVELOP AT AN INCREDIBLY FAST RATE AND SO NEED TO EAT LITTLE AND OFTEN TO SUSTAIN ENERGY AND GROWTH LEVELS.

AGAIN FOODS FROM THE PREVIOUS SECTIONS CAN STILL BE SERVED TO YOUR BABY; JUST ADJUST THE TEXTURES AS NECESSARY.

Suitable Foods

FOODS TO INCLUDE
- whole eggs
- finely ground nuts
- more flavourings – stock cubes if part of a family-size casserole

- greater selection of finger foods – slices of peeled fruit (such as dessert apple or pear), raw carrot and cucumber sticks, small squares of cooked chicken

- selection of foods from the four main food groups

Apple, carrot and cucumber

Left: *Finger foods – such as chopped raw vegetables and fruit pieces – come into their own at this age, and children love to help themselves.*

Whole egg

Above: *Inquisitive children love the time when they can join the family at the table.*

FOODS TO AVOID
- keep salt to a minimum and omit if possible
- sugar: add just enough to make the food appetizing without being overly sweet
- honey
- fat: trim visible fat off raw meat, grill rather than fry
- organ meats – liver, kidney

Below: *Though now a very small list, there are still some foods it is important to omit.*

Stock cubes

Ground nuts

I can feed myself!

Encouraging your baby to feed herself can be a truly messy business. Some babies are interested from a very early age and those little fingers seem to move like lightning grabbing the bowl or the spoon you're using to feed them with. While foods are still finely puréed, give your baby a second spoon to play with, leaving you more able to spoon in the real lunch.

As your baby grows offer her a few finger foods to hold and hopefully eat, while you continue to feed from a spoon. Cooked carrot sticks, broccoli and cauliflower florets are soft on a young mouth and easy to chew. As your baby grows so you can introduce bread sticks and toast fingers.

Encourage your baby to pick up foods and as her co-ordination improves and she gets the idea, so more food will actually go where it is intended. Try to cut down on the mess by rolling up your baby's sleeves and covering clothes with a large bib, preferably with sleeves.

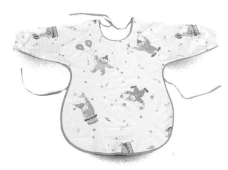

Above: *A bib with sleeves.*

Remove any hair bands and have a wet flannel at the ready.

Although it is tempting not to allow a baby feed herself, try not to be frustrated by the mess. Babies that are encouraged to feed themselves will probably be more adventurous later on and you will probably find there is less mess than

TEACHING YOUR BABY TO FEED ITSELF

1 Cover your baby well – this can be very messy! Give him a spoon of his own to play with.

2 While you are feeding your baby, allow him to play with the food – with his hands or the spoon.

3 Let your baby use the cup and spoon by himself. Don't worry about spillage – there are bound to be lots of slips at this stage.

4 Keep tissues or a damp flannel available and clean as you go. Be patient and take things slowly.

with a baby who is always spoon fed and keeps grabbing at the bowl. In addition, she will be able to join in your family meals and also give you the chance to eat your own meal before it goes cold.

WHAT TO DO IF YOUR CHILD CHOKES

● Don't waste time trying to remove food from your baby's mouth unless it can be done easily.
● Turn your baby, head down, supporting her head with your forearm and slap firmly between the shoulder blades.
● If this does not work, try again.
● Don't hesitate to ring your doctor or emergency services if worried.

Above: *Don't be afraid to take quick, firm action in an emergency.*

COPING WITH THE MESS

As babies grow so too does the amount of mess! It can seem incredible how just a few tablespoons of lunch can be spread across so many surfaces and so many items of clothing.
● Choose a large bib. Fabric bibs with a plastic liner are the most comfortable for babies to wear when tiny, moving on to a plastic pelican-style bib to catch the bits as they grow older. Check the back of your

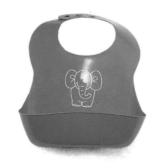

Above: *A hard plastic 'pelican' bib.*

baby's neck as these can rub.
● If you plan to feed your baby in the dining room, then protect the carpet with an old sheet, pieces of newspaper or plastic tablecloth or groundsheet. It is vital to take this with you if visiting friends.
● Give your baby a second spoon or small toy to play with so that she doesn't make a grab for the laden spoon.

Left: *It is a real delight when your baby can begin to feed independently. Not only can you start to eat with your baby, and relax a little more, but she will also enjoy setting her own pace and eating her meal in the order she chooses. At this stage the family can usually return to eating together around the table as a group.*

Above: *A plastic tablecloth or groundsheet on the floor will avoid carpet stains.*

FINGER FOODS

Finger foods are not only fun to eat but help your baby's co-ordination. Snacks play an important part in a young child's diet as appetites may be small, but energy and growth needs are great. Choose foods that are nutrient dense and avoid sweet sugary snacks such as chocolate biscuits.

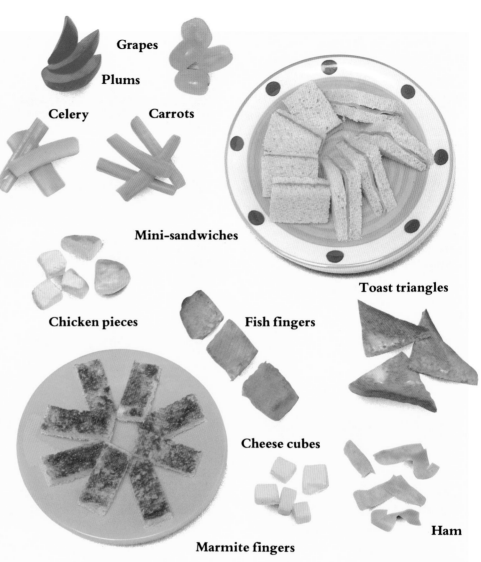

Grapes

Plums

Celery   **Carrots**

Mini-sandwiches

Toast triangles

Chicken pieces   **Fish fingers**

Cheese cubes

Marmite fingers

Ham

Above: *Your baby can eat at her own pace until she is full.*

TIPS

- Always make sure baby is comfortable either on your lap or strapped into a baby chair or highchair.
- Check the temperature of the food and make sure it is not too hot.
- Change the texture of the food: some babies like quite wet mixtures, some hate lumps, some like a few lumps for interest, others prefer food they can pick up – tiny ham sandwiches, thick slices of grilled fishfinger, even picking up peas and sweetcorn.
- Encourage your baby to feed herself; don't worry about mess – your baby is still learning – but just mop up sticky hands and face at the end.
- Try to keep calm. If your baby keeps spitting food out, you may find it less upsetting to offer bought food rather than homemade so you don't feel you've been wasting your time cooking.
- Try not to let your baby see you're upset or cross. Even a one-year-old can sense the power she can have over you.
- If solid meals are well established, give her a drink at the end of the meal so that she is not full up with milk before she begins.
- Avoid biscuits and sweet things as your baby will soon learn that if she makes a fuss when the savoury is offered, then pudding will soon follow.
- Remember no baby will starve herself. Continue offering a variety of food and don't despair.

Above: *Give drinks at the end of the meal, or they will fill your baby up before he eats.*

Coping with a fussy eater

All children are fussy eaters at some stage. If mealtimes are always calm and plates always clean then your family must be one in a million. Even very young children learn the power they have over their parents and mealtimes give them a great opportunity to exercise it. Here are some common problems and advice on how to deal with them.

BABY SPITS OUT FOOD

You may be trying to wean your baby too soon or possibly she simply doesn't like the taste of the food. If you started with baby rice then go on to potato or parsnip purée or a little apple purée mixed into the baby rice. If that fails, your baby may simply not be ready for solids yet. Try again in a week or two's time.

BABY APPEARS TO GAG

Some babies just cannot cope with solids at first and may seem distressed and almost gag on the food. Try thinning down the food with a little more formula milk or water, since the food may be too thick. Alternatively, you may be putting too much food on the spoon; try offering the baby a little less. If neither of these seem to help, stop solids and breast or bottle feed as usual, giving her plenty of reassuring cuddles. Try again in a few days' or weeks' time. If your baby is nearly six months old then ask your health visitor or doctor for advice.

BABY SEEMS TO HAVE A SMALL APPETITE

Babies' appetites, like adults', vary enormously. Don't force feed your baby; if she's been eating well and then turns her head away or starts spitting it out, it's a pretty clear indication that she's had enough, even if the amount does seem very small to you. Resist the temptation to encourage the baby to clear the dish: it is never helpful to force children of any age, and can be extremely counterproductive. If you're worried, talk to your health visitor and regularly check your baby's weight.

Above: *Don't worry when you encounter resistance in feeding: there never has been a baby that likes all foods, all the time.*

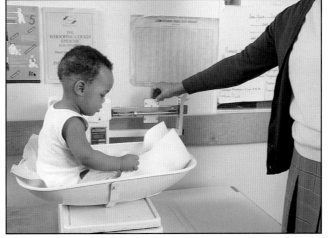

Left: *If you have serious anxieties, see your doctor or health visitor and get your baby's weight checked regularly.*

Going Vegetarian

A vegetarian diet can provide all the necessary nutrients for health and vitality, but it is important to balance the baby's diet to ensure that she receives adequate supplies of protein, vitamins D and B12, calcium and iron.

The basic guidelines are the same as for weaning any other baby; introduce flavours slowly and be guided by your baby. The biggest differences are obviously in the type of foods offered. Instead of obtaining protein from meat and fish, your baby will receive it from other protein-rich food. These include eggs, pulses, split lentils and grains, finely ground nuts or nut creams, sunflower seed spread, milk and dairy products and vegetarian cheese where available.

Vegetarians need to make sure that sufficient iron is included in their baby's diet. If she is over six months, offer prune juice, puréed apricots, molasses, refined lentils and cereals, particularly fortified breakfast cereals. Green vegetables and well-mashed beans, if over eight months, are also a good source of iron. Vitamin C aids absorption of iron from plant sources so make sure you serve fresh green vegetables or fruit in the meal. Your doctor may also feel it beneficial for your baby to take vitamin drops.

If you plan to bring the baby up as a vegan and so omit dairy products and eggs from the diet, then it is vital

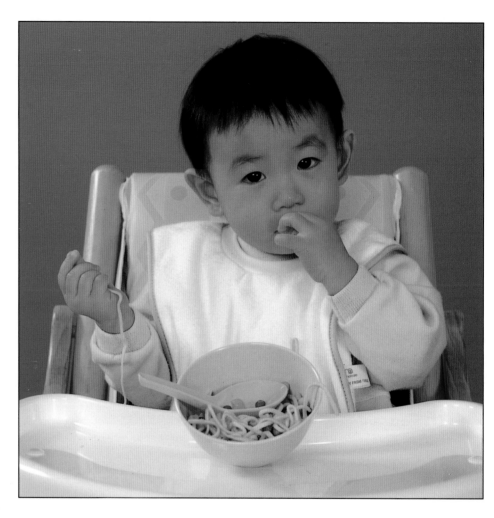

to consult your doctor or dietician.

Vegetarian diets tend to be bulky and lower in calories than a diet containing meats so make sure you include foods which are protein and calorie rich, with little or no fibre, such as eggs, milk and cheese. These can be mixed with smaller quantities of vegetables, fruit and cereals. Fibre-rich foods can also be difficult

Above: *Raising your child as a vegetarian takes special planning and care.*

for a child to digest as many nutrients may pass straight through.

To ensure your baby is getting the correct amount of vitamins, minerals and food energy her diet should include foods from the four groups on the opposite page:

Oranges

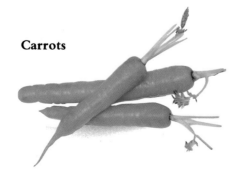
Carrots

Cucumber

Grapes

Cereals and grains: rice around four months; pasta, bread, oats, and breakfast cereals from six months.

Fruit and vegetables: begin with potato, carrot, apple and pear around four months, progressing to stronger-flavoured foods as your baby develops.

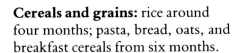

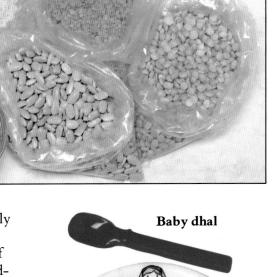

Dairy produce: including milk, cheese, fromage frais and yogurt from six months.
Note: Make sure cheese is rennet-free. If you are unsure, ask the delicatessen assistant, or check the packet if pre-packed.

Beans and pulses: split and softly cooked lentils from five or six months. Gradual introduction of tofu, smooth peanut butter, hard-boiled egg yolks from six months. Well cooked mashed dried beans and peas and finely ground nuts from nine months. Do not give whole nuts to the under fives.

To make sure your baby is thriving and happy, irrespective of the type of diet, make sure you check your baby's weight at regular intervals at the health clinic.

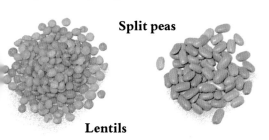

Split peas

Lentils

Baby dhal

The Importance of a Varied Diet

Once your baby progresses to more varied fruit and vegetable purées, you are really beginning to lay down the foundations for a healthy eating pattern and sound nutritional habits which will take your baby through childhood and into adult life.

It is vitally important to include portions of food from each of the four main food groups per day. But do make sure that the types of food you choose are suitable for the age of your child.

Left: Your baby is now at the age where the diet can and should be as diverse as any adult's. Variety is crucial for health reasons, and also has the benefit of allowing you many options for tempting and maintaining the kind of interest in all types of food that will ensure good eating habits develop for the future.

Group 1: *Cereals, bread, potatoes, rice and pasta*

Group 2: *Fruit and vegetables* – bland tastes to start, such as potato, swede and parsnip, then stronger flavours and a wider variety

Group 3: *Meat and meat alternatives* – meat, poultry, fish, eggs, pulses (peas, beans and lentils), tofu, finely ground nuts

Group 4: *Milk and milk products* – milk, including soya milk, cheese, yogurt (plain at first, then flavoured), fromage frais

There are two more food groups which add palatability to the diet as well as contributing energy.

Group 5: *Sugars*

Group 6: *Fats and oils*

It is not recommended you add sugar to baby foods or give lots of sugary drinks, particularly in the early days of weaning. Many of us have an inherent need for sweetness but to cater to this without building in bad habits try and include foods in the diet that are naturally sweet. Choose dessert apples instead of very sharp cooking apples, mix bananas or ripe apricots with sharper-tasting fruits.

For those foods that are very sharp try and add 5ml/1tsp sugar per portion, so they become palatable without being overly sweet. Given the choice your baby would prefer sweet flavours to savoury so make sure you include a good range of tastes in the diet. Too much sugar or sweetened foods or drinks at this stage could lead to tooth decay before the teeth are even through.

Try to avoid offering biscuits as a mid-morning or afternoon snack. Try to encourage your baby to eat:
- a piece of banana
- a plain bread roll
- a few triangles of marmite toast
- a milky drink
- a small pot of fromage frais

Watch the amounts of fat and oil you include in the diet. Avoid frying especially when preparing first foods as young babies have difficulty digesting such foods. As your baby develops, you can spread toast fingers with a little butter or margarine or offer a few oven-baked chips as easy-to-hold finger foods. Maintain the milk feeds and introduce cows' milk (full-fat) after one year as the main drink of the day. Don't be tempted to serve skimmed milk as the valuable fat-soluble vitamins A and D will be lost, and your baby may not get the energy needed for growth.

HOMEMADE OR MANUFACTURED FOODS?
Most mothers use a combination of the two. Bought baby foods are convenient and often easier to use if going out for the day or until your baby's meals coincide with the rest

Above: *A piece of fruit or chopped vegetable is always preferable to a biscuit.*

of the family. Dried baby foods can be useful in the very early days when baby is eating only a teaspoon of food at each meal. On the other hand, homemade foods can be batch cooked or made with some of the ingredients from the main family meal and are often less trouble than you would expect. Added to this is the satisfaction of knowing your baby has eaten a wholesome meal and hopefully is acquiring a taste for home cooking.

Left: *Don't always assume that all homemade foods are better and more nutritional than all manufactured foods. There are now some excellent products available for purchase which can save you time and effort and add hugely to your repertoire without any loss of dietary values.*

Lamb Couscous

Makes: 750ml/1⅓ pint/3⅓ cups

115g/4oz carrot
115g/4oz swede
¼ onion
175g/6oz lamb fillet
5ml/1 tsp oil
10ml/2 tsp vegetable purée
30ml/2 tbsp currants
300ml/½ pint/1¼ cups water
50g/2oz couscous

1 Peel the carrot, swede and onion, rinse and chop. Rinse the lamb, trim off any fat, and chop.

2 Heat the oil in a saucepan, and fry the lamb until browned.

3 Add the vegetables, cook for 2 minutes then stir in the vegetable purée, currants and water. Cover and simmer for 25 minutes.

4 Rinse the couscous in a sieve. Cover and steam the couscous over the lamb pan, for 5 minutes.

5 Chop or process the lamb mixture to the desired consistency. Fluff up the couscous with a fork and add to the lamb mixture stirring well.

6 Spoon a little into a bowl, test the temperature and cool if necessary, before giving to baby.

7 Cover the remaining food and transfer to the fridge as soon as possible. Use within 24 hours.

- Suitable for freezing.

TIP
Look out for vegetable purée in tubes on the same shelf as the tomato purée in the supermarket.

Paprika Pork

Makes: 600ml/1 pint/2½ cups

175g/6oz lean pork
75g/3oz carrot
175g/6oz potato
¼ onion
¼ red pepper
5ml/1tsp oil
2.5ml/½ tsp paprika
150g/5oz/⅔ cup baked beans
150ml/¼ pint/⅔ cup water

1 Preheat the oven to 180°C/ 350°F/Gas 4. Rinse the pork under cold water, pat dry and trim away any fat or gristle. Cut the pork into small cubes.

2 Peel the carrot, potato and onion. Cut away the core and remove any seeds from the pepper. Put into a colander, rinse under cold water then chop into small pieces.

3 Heat the oil in a flameproof casserole, add the pork and fry for a few minutes, stirring until browned. Add the vegetables, cook for 2 minutes then add the paprika, baked beans and water.

4 Bring back to the boil, then cover and cook in the oven for 1¼ hours until the pork is tender.

5 Chop or process the casserole to the desired consistency, then spoon a little into a bowl. Test the temperature and cool if necessary, before giving to baby.

6 Cover the remaining food and transfer to the fridge as soon as possible. Use within 24 hours.

● Suitable for freezing.

TIP
If using a food processor to chop baby dinner, drain off most of the liquid. Process then stir in liquid until desired texture is reached.

Chicken and Celery Supper

Makes: 600ml/1 pint/2½ cups

175g/6oz chicken thighs, skinned and boned
¼ onion
225g/8oz carrots
75g/3oz celery
5ml/1 tsp oil
10ml/2 tsp vegetable puree
250ml/8fl oz/1 cup water

1 Rinse the chicken under cold water, pat dry, trim off any fat and cut into chunks.

2 Trim and rinse the vegetables and cut into small pieces.

3 Heat the oil in a saucepan, add the chicken and onion and fry for a few minutes, stirring until browned. Add the carrots, celery, vegetable purée and water. Bring to the boil, cover and simmer for 20 minutes until tender.

4 Chop or process the mixture to the desired consistency. If using a food processor, process the solids first and then add the liquid a little at a time.

5 Spoon a little into a bowl, test the temperature and cool if necessary, before giving to baby.

6 Cover the remaining casserole and transfer to the fridge as soon as possible. Use within 24 hours.

● Suitable for freezing.

TIP
For extra flavour, add homemade stock instead of the water, or use commercial stock, but make sure it does not have a high sodium level.

Cauliflower and Broccoli Cheese

Makes: 600ml/1 pint/2½ cups

175g/6oz cauliflower

175g/6oz broccoli

175g/6oz potato

300ml/½ pint/1¼ cups formula milk

75g/3oz mild Cheddar cheese

1 Rinse the vegetables, then break the cauliflower and broccoli into florets. Slice the tender stems but cut out and discard any woody core from the cauliflower. Peel and chop the potatoes into cubes.

2 Place the vegetables and milk in a saucepan, bring to the boil, cover and simmer for 12–15 minutes until quite tender.

3 Grate the cheese and add to the vegetables stirring until the cheese has melted.

4 Process or mash the mixture to the desired consistency, adding a little extra milk if necessary.

5 Spoon a little into a bowl, test the temperature and cool if necessary, before serving to baby.

6 Cover the remaining food and transfer to the fridge as soon as possible. Use within 24 hours.

● Suitable for freezing.

Cheesy Tagliatelle with Broccoli and Ham

Makes: 600ml/1 pint/2½ cups

| 115g/4oz broccoli |
| 50g/2oz wafer thin ham |
| 50g/2oz Cheddar cheese |
| 300ml/½ pint/1¼ cups formula milk |
| 50g/2oz tagliatelle |

1 Rinse the broccoli and cut into small florets, chopping the stalks. Chop the ham and grate the Cheddar cheese.

2 Pour the formula milk into a saucepan, bring to the boil and add the tagliatelle. Simmer uncovered for 5 minutes.

3 Add the broccoli and cook for 10 minutes until tender.

TIP
Pasta swells on standing so you may need to thin the cooled leftover mixture with extra formula milk before reheating.

4 Add the ham and cheese to the broccoli and pasta, stirring until the cheese has melted.

5 Chop or process the mixture to the desired consistency and then spoon a little into a bowl. Test the temperature and cool if necessary, before giving to baby.

6 Cover the remaining food and transfer to the fridge as soon as possible. Use within 24 hours.

● Suitable for freezing.

Baby Dahl

Makes: 600ml/1 pint/2½ cups

50g/2oz/¼ cup red lentils
¼ onion
2.5ml/½ tsp ground coriander
1.25ml/¼ tsp turmeric
350ml/12fl oz/1½ cups water
75g/3oz potato
75g/3oz carrot
75g/3oz cauliflower
75g/3oz green cabbage

1 Rinse the lentils under cold water, discarding any black bits.

2 Chop onion, add to saucepan with lentils, spices and water.

3 Bring to the boil, cover and simmer for 20 minutes.

4 Chop the potato, carrot and cabbage. Break the cauliflower into small florets.

5 Stir the vegetables into the pan. Cook for 12–15 minutes.

6 Chop or process the dahl to the desired consistency, adding a little extra boiled water if necessary.

7 Spoon a little dahl into a bowl, test the temperature and cool if necessary, before serving to baby.

8 Cover the remaining dahl and transfer to the fridge as soon as possible. Use within 24 hours.

• Suitable for freezing.

Cheesy Fish Pie

Makes: 450ml/¾ pint/1⅞ cups

225g/8oz potato

50g/2oz leek

50g/2oz button mushrooms

90g/3½oz brick frozen skinless cod

250ml/8fl oz/1 cup formula milk

50g/2oz Cheddar cheese, grated

1 Peel the potato, halve the leek and trim the mushrooms. Place all the vegetables in a colander and rinse well with cold water, drain, then chop the vegetables.

2 Place the vegetables in a saucepan with the frozen fish and milk. Bring to the boil, cover and simmer for 15 minutes, until the fish is cooked and the potatoes are tender when pierced with a knife.

3 Lift the fish out of pan with a slotted spoon and break into pieces with a knife and fork checking carefully for bones.

4 Return the fish to the pan and stir in the grated cheese. Chop or process the mixture to give the desired consistency.

5 Spoon a little into a bowl, test the temperature and cool if necessary, before serving to baby.

6 Cover the remaining fish pie and transfer to the fridge as soon as possible. Use within 24 hours.

• Suitable for freezing.

Fish Creole

Makes: 450ml/¾ pint/1⅞ cups

50g/2oz celery

50g/2oz red pepper

300ml/½ pint/1¼ cups water

50g/2oz/¼ cup long grain rice

10ml/2 tsp tomato ketchup

90g/3¼oz brick frozen skinless cod

1   Trim the celery and discard the core and seeds from the pepper. Rinse and chop the vegetables.

2   Bring the water to the boil in a saucepan and add the vegetables, rice, ketchup and fish.

3   Bring back to the boil, then reduce heat, cover and simmer for 15 minutes, until the rice is tender and the fish is cooked.

4   Lift the fish out of the pan with a slotted spoon. Use a knife and fork to check for bones.

5   Stir the fish back into the pan and then chop or process.

6   Spoon a little fish mixture into a small bowl, test the temperature and cool if necessary, before giving to baby.

7   Cover the leftover fish creole and transfer to the fridge as soon as possible. Use within 24 hours.

● Suitable for freezing.

Chocolate Pots

Makes: 2

5ml/1 tsp cocoa
5ml/1 tsp caster sugar
150ml/¼ pint/⅔ cup formula or cows' milk
1 egg

1 Preheat the oven to 180°C/ 350°F/Gas 4. Blend the cocoa and sugar with a little of the milk in a small bowl to make a smooth paste. Stir in the remaining milk and then pour the mixture into a saucepan.

2 Bring just to the boil. Beat the egg in a bowl then gradually stir in the hot milk, mixing well until the mixture is smooth.

3 Strain the mixture into two ramekin dishes to remove any egg solids.

4 Place the dishes in a roasting tin or shallow cake tin. Pour boiling water into the tin to come halfway up the sides of the dishes.

5 Cook in the oven for 15–20 minutes or until the custard has set. Leave to cool.

6 Transfer to the fridge as soon as possible. Serve one pudding and use the second within 24 hours.

Vanilla Custards

Makes: 2

1 egg

5ml/1 tsp caster sugar

few drops vanilla essence

150ml/¼ pint/⅔ cup formula or
   cows' milk

1 Preheat the oven to 180°C/
350°F/Gas 4. Using a fork, beat
the egg, sugar and vanilla essence
together in a bowl.

2 Pour the milk into a small
saucepan and heat until it is just
to the boil.

4 Strain into two ramekin dishes
and place in a roasting tin. Add
enough boiling water to come
halfway up the sides of the dishes.

3 Gradually stir the milk into the
egg mixture, whisking or
beating until smooth.

5 Bake for 15–20 minutes or until
the custard has set. Cool and
serve as for **Chocolate Pots**.

Marmite Bread Sticks

Makes: 36

little oil, for greasing

150g/5oz packet pizza base mix

flour, for dusting

5ml/1 tsp Marmite

1 egg yolk

1 Brush two baking sheets with a little oil. Put the pizza mix in a bowl, add the quantity of water as directed on the packet and mix to make a smooth dough.

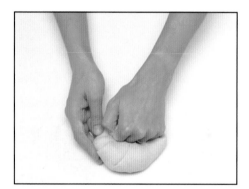

2 Knead on a lightly floured surface for 5 minutes until smooth and elastic.

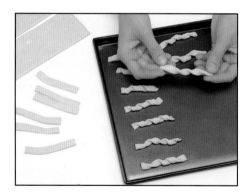

3 Roll out to a 23cm/9in square. Cut into strips 7.5cm × 1cm/3 × ½in, twisting each to give a corkscrew effect. Arrange on the baking sheets, slightly spaced apart.

4 Mix the Marmite and egg yolk together and brush over the bread sticks. Loosely cover with oiled clear film and leave in a warm place for 20–30 minutes to rise.

5 Meanwhile preheat the oven to 220°C/425°F/Gas 7. Bake the bread sticks for 8–10 minutes until well risen. Loosen but leave to cool on the baking sheet.

6 Serve one or two sticks to baby. Store the rest in a plastic box for up to three days.

● Suitable for freezing up to three months in a plastic bag.

Eggy Bread Fingers

Makes: 16

2 slices bread

1 egg

30ml/2 tbsp formula or cows' milk

little butter and oil, for frying

1 Trim the crusts off the bread, then cut each slice in half.

2 Beat the egg and milk in a shallow dish and dip the bread, one slice at a time, into the egg until coated on both sides.

3 Heat a little butter and oil in a frying pan. Add the bread and fry until browned on both sides.

4 Cool slightly, cut into fingers and serve to baby as finger food or as part of a meal.

Cheese Straws

Makes: 42

little oil for greasing

175g/6oz/1½ cups plain flour

75g/3oz/6 tbsp butter or margarine, cut into pieces

115g/4oz Cheddar cheese, grated

1 egg, beaten

1 Preheat the oven to 200°C/ 400°F/Gas 6. Brush two baking sheets lightly with oil.

2 Place the flour in a bowl, add the butter or margarine and rub in until the mixture resembles fine breadcrumbs. Stir in the grated Cheddar cheese.

3 Reserve 15ml/1 tbsp beaten egg and then stir the rest into the pastry mixture. Mix to a smooth dough, adding water if necessary.

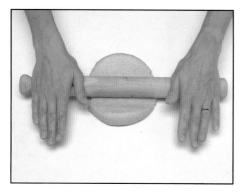

4 Knead lightly and roll out on a floured surface to a rectangle 30 × 20cm/12 × 8in. Brush with remaining egg.

5 Cut into strips 7.5 × 1cm/ 3 × ½in and place on the baking sheets, spaced slightly apart.

6 Bake in the oven for 8–10 minutes until golden brown. Loosen from but leave to cool on the baking sheets.

7 Serve one or two sticks to baby and store the rest in a plastic box for up to 1 week.

● Suitable for freezing up to three months in a plastic box, interleaved with greaseproof paper.

TIP
Begin making these with mild cheese and as your child gets more adventurous change to stronger flavoured cheese.

Mini Cup Cakes

Makes: 26

50g/2oz/4 tbsp soft margarine
50g/2oz/¼ cup caster sugar
50g/2oz/⅓ cup self-raising flour
1 egg

1 Preheat the oven to 180°C/ 350°F/Gas 4. Separate 26 paper mini muffin cases and place on a large baking sheet.

2 Put all the ingredients for the cake into a mixing bowl and beat together well until smooth.

3 Divide the mixture among the cases and cook for 8–10 minutes until well risen and golden.

4 Transfer cakes to a wire rack and leave to cool completely, then peel the paper off one or two cakes and serve to baby.

5 Store the remaining cakes in a plastic box for up to three days.

● Suitable for freezing up to three months in a plastic box.

TIP
Cut a cup cake in half crossways and spread one half with a little sugar-free jam. Replace top half and serve to baby.

Shortbread Shapes

Makes: 60

little oil, for greasing
150g/5oz/1 cup plain flour
25g/1oz/3 tbsp cornflour
50g/2oz/¼ cup caster sugar
115g/4oz/½ cup butter
extra sugar, for sprinkling (optional)

1 Preheat the oven to 180°C/
350°F/Gas 4. Brush two baking
sheets with a little oil.

2 Put the flour, cornflour and
sugar in a bowl. Cut the butter
into pieces and rub into the flour
until the mixture resembles fine
breadcrumbs. Mould to a dough
with your hands.

3 Knead lightly and roll out on a
floured surface to a 5mm/¼in
thickness. Stamp out shapes with
small biscuit or petits fours cutters.

4 Transfer to the baking sheets,
sprinkle with extra sugar, if
liked, and cook for 10–12 minutes
until pale golden. Loosen with a
knife and leave to cool on the baking
sheets, then transfer to a wire rack.

5 Offer baby one or two shapes
and store the rest in a plastic box
for up to one week.

TIP
These biscuits will keep well in the
freezer for three months. Pack in
rigid plastic boxes and thaw in a
single layer. If you prefer, you can
freeze the biscuits before baking.
Wrap well to prevent them taking
up flavours from other food.

STAGE 5: FROM BABY TO TODDLER

ONCE YOUR CHILD HAS REACHED 12 MONTHS HE OR SHE WILL BE ENJOYING A VARIED DIET AND VERY DEFINITE PERSONAL FOOD PREFERENCES WILL BE DEVELOPING. THIS IS ALSO A TIME WHEN FUSSY EATING HABITS MAY APPEAR. REMEMBER THAT A TODDLER'S APPETITE VARIES ENORMOUSLY AND YOU MAY FIND THAT HE OR SHE WILL EAT VERY WELL ONE DAY AND EAT HARDLY ANYTHING THE NEXT. BE GUIDED BY YOUR TODDLER AND TRY TO THINK IN TERMS OF WHAT THE CHILD HAS EATEN OVER SEVERAL DAYS RATHER THAN WORRYING ABOUT WHAT THEY DON'T EAT ON ONE DAY.

IN THIS SECTION YOU WILL FIND SOME FAVOURITE BABY RECIPES FROM THE EARLIER STAGES UPDATED FOR YOUR GROWING TODDLER.

FOODS TO INCLUDE

Give your child a selection of foods in the four main food groups daily:

Cereal and filler foods: include three to four helpings of the following per day – breakfast cereals, bread, pasta, potatoes, rice.

Fruit and vegetables: try to provide three or four helpings per day. Choose from fresh, canned, frozen or dried.

Meat and/or alternatives: one to two portions per day – meat – all kinds, including burgers and sausages, poultry, fish (fresh, canned or frozen), eggs (well-cooked), lentils and pulses (for example baked beans, red kidney beans, chick-peas), finely chopped nuts, smooth peanut butter, seeds, tofu, and Quorn.

Dairy foods: include 600ml/1 pint of milk per day or a mix of milk, cheese, yogurt and fromage frais. For a child who goes off drinking milk, try flavouring it or using it in custards, ice cream, rice pudding or cheese sauce. A carton of yogurt or 40g/1½oz of cheese have the same amount of calcium as 190ml/⅓ pint of milk.

Above: *Cereal and filler foods, like bread, pasta and rice.*

Above: *Fruit and vegetables, including frozen, dried and canned goods.*

Above: *Meat and meat alternatives, like pulses and nuts.*

Above: *Dairy foods such as milk, cheese and yogurt.*

Saucy Ham Pasta

Serves 2

50g/2oz dried pasta shapes

50g/2oz/½ cup frozen mixed
   vegetables

30ml/2 tbsp margarine

30ml/2 tbsp plain flour

150ml/¼ pint/⅔ cup milk

50g/2oz/½ cup grated red Leicester
   or Cheddar cheese

2 slices ham, chopped

salt and pepper

3 Stir two-thirds of the grated
cheese into the sauce and add the
drained pasta and vegetables, the
ham and a little salt and pepper.

4 Spoon into two shallow dishes
and sprinkle with the remaining
cheese. Cool slightly if necessary.

TIP
This recipe also works well if you
use a 100g/3½oz can tuna, drained,
in place of the ham. You could
serve the ham and vegetable sauce
with rice, if you prefer.

1 Cook the pasta in a saucepan of
boiling water for 5 minutes.
Add vegetables and cook for 5 more
minutes until pasta is tender. Drain.

2 Melt the margarine in a
medium-sized pan and stir in the
flour. Gradually add the milk and
bring to the boil, stirring, until the
sauce is thickened and smooth.

Shepherds' Pie

Serves 2

½ small onion

175g/6oz lean minced beef

10ml/2 tsp plain flour

30ml/2 tbsp tomato ketchup

150ml/¼ pint/⅔ cup beef stock

pinch of mixed herbs

slice swede, about 50g/2oz

½ small parsnip, about 50g/2oz

1 medium-sized potato, about 115g/
4oz

10ml/2 tsp milk

15g/½oz/1 tbsp butter or margarine

½ carrot

40g/1½oz/3 tbsp frozen peas

salt and pepper (optional)

1 Preheat oven to 190°C/375°F/
Gas 5. Finely chop the onion,
and place in a small saucepan with
the mince and dry fry over a low
heat, stirring, until the mince is
evenly browned.

5 Spoon the mince into two
250ml/8fl oz/1 cup ovenproof
dishes. Place the mashed vegetables
on top fluffing them up with a fork.
Dot with butter or margarine.

6 Place both the pies on a baking
sheet and cook for about 25–30
minutes until browned on top
and bubbly.

7 Peel and thinly slice the carrot
lengthways. Stamp out shapes
with petits fours cutters. Cook in a
saucepan of boiling water with the
peas for 5 minutes. Drain and serve
with the shepherds' pies. Remember
that baked pies are very hot when
they come out of the oven. Always
allow to cool slightly before serving
to children.

2 Add the flour, stirring, then add
the ketchup, stock, mixed herbs
and seasoning, if liked. Bring to the
boil, cover and simmer gently for 30
minutes, stirring occasionally.

3 Meanwhile, chop the swede,
parsnip and potato and cook for
20 minutes until tender. Drain.

4 Mash with the milk and half of
the butter or margarine.

Lamb Stew

Serves 2

115g/4oz lamb fillet
¼ small onion
1 small carrot, about 50g/2oz
½ small parsnip, about 50g/2oz
1 small potato
5ml/1 tsp oil
150ml/¼ pint/⅔ cup lamb stock
pinch of dried rosemary
salt and pepper (optional)
crusty bread, to serve

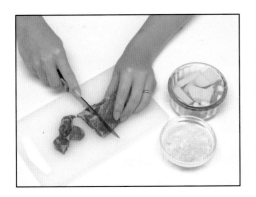

1 Rinse the lamb under cold water and pat dry. Cut away any fat from the meat and cut into small cubes. Finely chop the onion, then dice the carrot and parsnip and cut the potato into slightly larger pieces.

2 Heat the oil in a medium-size saucepan, add the lamb and onion and fry gently until browned. Add the carrot, parsnip and potato and fry the lamb and vegetables for a further 3 minutes, stirring.

3 Add the lamb stock, dried rosemary and a little salt and pepper, if liked. Bring to the boil, cover and simmer for 35–40 minutes or until the meat is tender and moist.

4 Spoon the stew into shallow bowls and cool slightly before serving with crusty bread.

Cheesy Fish Pies

Serves 2

1 medium-sized potato, about 150g/5oz

25g/1oz green cabbage

115g/4oz cod or hoki fillets

25g/1oz/2 tbsp frozen sweetcorn

150ml/¼ pint/⅔ cup milk

15ml/1 tbsp butter or margarine

15ml/1 tbsp plain flour

25g/1oz/¼ cup grated red Leicester cheese

5ml/1 tsp sesame seeds

carrots and mange tout, to serve

4 Strain the fish and sweetcorn, reserving the cooking liquid. Wash the pan then melt the butter or margarine in the pan. Stir in the flour then gradually add the reserved cooking liquid and bring to the boil, stirring until thickened and smooth.

5 Add the fish and sweetcorn with half of the grated cheese. Spoon into two small ovenproof dishes.

6 Mash the potato and cabbage with the remaining 10ml/2 tsp milk. Stir in half of the remaining cheese and spoon the mixture over the fish. Sprinkle with the sesame seeds and the remaining cheese.

7 Cook under a preheated grill until the topping is browned. Cool slightly before serving with vegetable fishes.

1 Peel and cut the potato into chunks and shred the cabbage. Cut any skin away from the fish fillets and rinse under cold water.

2 Bring a saucepan of water to the boil, add the potato and cook for 10 minutes. Add the cabbage and cook for a further 5 minutes until tender. Drain.

3 Meanwhile place the fish fillets, the sweetcorn and all but 10ml/2 tsp of the milk in a second saucepan. Bring to the boil then cover the saucepan and simmer very gently for 8–10 minutes until the fish flakes easily when pressed with a knife.

Broccoli and Cauliflower Cheese

Serves 2

1 egg
75g/3oz broccoli
75g/3oz cauliflower
15g/½oz/1 tbsp margarine
15ml/1 tbsp plain flour
150ml/¼ pint/⅔ cup milk
40g/1½oz/⅓ cup grated red Leicester cheese
½ tomato
salt and pepper (optional)

1 Put the egg in a small saucepan of cold water, bring to the boil and cook for about 10 minutes until the egg is hard-boiled.

2 Meanwhile cut the broccoli and cauliflower into florets and thinly slice the broccoli stalks. Cook in a saucepan of boiling water for about 8 minutes until just tender.

3 Drain the vegetables and dry the pan. Melt the margarine, stir in the flour then gradually mix in the milk and bring to the boil, stirring until thickened and smooth.

TIP
Making a face or fun pattern can be just enough to tempt a fussy eater to try something new.

4 Stir two-thirds of the cheese into the sauce together with a little seasoning, if liked. Reserve two of the broccoli florets and stir the remaining vegetables into the sauce.

5 Divide the mixture between two heat-resistant shallow dishes and sprinkle with the remaining cheese.

6 Place under a hot grill until golden brown and bubbling.

7 Make a face on each dish with broccoli florets for a nose, a halved tomato for a mouth and peeled and sliced hard-boiled egg for eyes. Cool slightly before serving.

Eggy Bread Butterflies

Serves 2

4 small broccoli florets
8 peas
1 small carrot
1 slice red Leicester or Cheddar cheese
2 slices ham
2 slices bread
1 egg
10ml/2 tsp milk
5ml/1 tsp sunflower oil
a little tomato ketchup

1 Cook the broccoli florets and the peas in a saucepan of boiling water for 5 minutes. Drain well.

2 For each butterfly, cut four thin slices of carrot and cut into flower shapes with a petits four cutter. Cut out four small squares from the cheese.

3 Cut four thin strips from the rest of the carrot for antennae. Roll up each piece of ham and arrange in the middle of two serving plates, to make the two butterfly bodies.

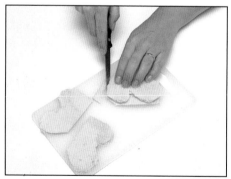

4 Cut butterfly wings from the bread using a small knife.

TIP
Vary the ingredients for butterfly decorations. Make a body from a grilled sausage if preferred.

5 Beat together the egg and milk and dip the bread in to coat both sides thoroughly. Heat the oil in a medium-sized frying pan and fry the bread until golden on both sides.

6 Assemble the butterfly, using the eggy bread for the wings and decorating with the carrot, cheese, broccoli and peas. Use a blob of ketchup for the head.

Pizza Clock

Serves 3–4

20cm/8in ready-made pizza base

45ml/3 tbsp tomato ketchup or pizza
  sauce

2 tomatoes

75g/3oz/¾ cup grated cheese

pinch of dried marjoram

1 green pepper

1 large carrot

1 thick slice ham

3 Meanwhile halve the pepper, cut away the core and seeds and stamp out the numbers 3, 6, 9 and 12 with small number cutters. Peel and thinly cut the carrot lengthways and stamp out the numbers 1, 2, 4, 5, 7, 8, 10 and 11. Arrange on the pizza to form a clock face.

4 Cut out a carrot circle. Cut two clock hands, each about 7.5cm/3in long from the ham. Arrange on the pizza with the round of carrot.

5 Place the pizza clock on to a serving plate and arrange the numbers around the edge. Cool the pizza clock slightly before cutting into wedges and serving.

1 Preheat oven to 220°C/425°F/ Gas 7. Place the pizza base on a baking sheet and spread with ketchup or pizza sauce. Chop the tomatoes and scatter over the pizza with the cheese and marjoram.

2 Place directly on an oven shelf and bake for 12 minutes, until the cheese is bubbly. (Place a baking tray on the shelf below the pizza to catch any drips of cheese.)

TIP

If preferred, make a smaller version of this using half a toasted muffin. Top as above and grill until the cheese melts. Add ham hands and small pieces of carrot to mark the numbers.

Pancakes

Serves 2–3

50g/2oz/⅓ cup plain flour

1 egg

150ml/¼ pint/⅔ cup milk

15ml/1 tbsp sunflower oil

For the filling

1 banana

1 orange

2–3 scoops ice cream

a little maple syrup

1 Sift the flour into a bowl, add the egg and gradually whisk in the milk to form a smooth batter. Whisk in 5ml/1 tsp of the oil.

2 To make the filling, slice the banana thinly or in chunks. Cut the peel away from the orange with a serrated knife, then cut the orange into segments.

3 Heat a little of the remaining oil in medium-sized non-stick pan, pour off any excess oil and add 30ml/2 tbsp of the batter. Tilt the pan to evenly coat the pan and cook for a couple of minutes until the pancake is set and the underside is golden.

4 Loosen the edges with a knife then toss the pancake or turn with a knife. Brown the other side and then slide out on to a plate. Fold in four and keep warm.

5 Cook the rest of the batter in the same way until you have made 6 pancakes. Place two on each plate.

6 Spoon a little fruit into each pancake and arrange on serving plates. Top with the remaining fruit, a scoop of ice cream and pour over a little maple syrup. Serve at once.

Raspberry Sorbet

Makes: 900ml/1½ pints/3¾ cups

10ml/2 tsp powdered gelatine

600ml/1 pint/2½ cups water

225g/8oz/1¼ cups caster sugar

675g/1½lb raspberries, hulled

grated rind and juice of ½ lemon

1 Put 30ml/2 tbsp water in a cup, sprinkle the gelatine over and set aside for a few minutes to soak.

2 Place the water and sugar in a saucepan and heat, stirring occasionally until the sugar has completely dissolved.

3 Bring to the boil and boil rapidly for 3 minutes. Remove from the heat, add the gelatine mixture to the syrup and stir until completely dissolved. Leave to cool.

4 Liquidize or process the raspberries to a smooth purée then press through a sieve into the syrup. Stir in lemon rind and juice.

5 Pour into a plastic tub and freeze for 6–7 hours or until the mixture is half frozen.

6 Beat the sorbet with a fork or transfer to a food processor and process until smooth. Return to the freezer and freeze until solid.

7 Remove the sorbet from the freezer 10 minutes before serving to soften slightly, then scoop into dishes with a melon baller or small teaspoon.

VARIATION
Summer Fruit Sorbet
Follow the recipe up to Step 3. Put a 500g/1¼lb pack of frozen summer fruits into a second saucepan. Add 60ml/4 tbsp water, cover and cook for 5 minutes until soft, then purée and sieve, add to the syrup and continue as above.

INDEX

ACKNOWLEDGEMENTS

The author and publishers would like to thank the following
for their contribution to this book:
- In particular, the Department of Health
for reading and approving the text.
- National Dairy Council Nutrition Service
- Health Education Authority
- Dr Nigel Dickie from Heinz Baby Foods
- The British Dietetic Association
- The Health Visitors' Association
- Broadstone Communications for their invaluable help
supplying the Kenwood equipment for recipe testing
and photography
- Hand-painted china plates, bowls and mugs from
Cosmo Place Studio, 11 Cosmo Place, London WC1N 3AP;
(0171 278 3374)
- Tupperware for plain-coloured plastic bowls, plates, feeder
beakers and cups
- Cole and Mason for non-breakable children's ware
- Royal Doulton for Bunnykins china
- Spode for blue and white Edwardian Childhood china

The publishers would like to thank the following children and
adults for being such wonderful models: Maurice Bishop,
Andrew Brown, Penny and Chloe Brown, Daisy May Bryant,
April Cane, Helen and Matthew Coates, Cameron Gillis,
Jamie Grant, Sandra and George Hadfield, Ted Howard
Emily Johnson, Huw and Rhees Jones, Kay, Stephen, Charlie
and Genevive Riddle, William Lewis, Sadé Walsh, Lionel and
Lucy Watson, Lily May Whitfield, Philippa Wish, James Wyatt.

PICTURE CREDITS
The publishers would like to thank the following for additional
images of babies used in the book:

Key: t = top; b = bottom; l = left; r = right.

Bubbles: pages 10 br (Jacqui Farrow); pages 21 t, 37, 67 tr (Lois
Joy Thurston); page 27 t (F Rombout); page 75 (S Price).
Lupe Cunha: pages 10 bl, 34/35, 40, 43 t, 56, 64, 73.
Greg Evans: page 80.
Sally and Richard Greenhill: page 62 t.
Lyons Waddell: page 59 t.
Reflections/Jennie Woodcock: pages 63 b, 66 tr, 76/77, 79, 87.
Timothy Woodcock: pages 10 t.